# the magical properties of workshop learning

studien zur berufs- und weiterbildung
studies in vocational and continuing education

band / vol. 2

herausgegeben von / edited by
philipp gonon & anja heikkinen

peter lang
bern · berlin · bruxelles · frankfurt am main · new york · oxford · wien

liv mjelde

# the magical properties of workshop learning

translated by
richard daly

peter lang
bern • berlin • bruxelles • frankfurt am main • new york • oxford • wien

**Bibliographic information published by Die Deutsche Bibliothek**
Die Deutsche Bibliothek lists this publication in the Deutsche Nationalbibliografie; detailed bibliographic data is available on the Internet at <http://dnb.ddb.de>.

British Library and Library of Congress Cataloguing-in-Publication Data:
A catalogue record for this book is available from The British Library, Great Britain, and from The Library of Congress, USA

This translation has been published with the financial support of the Foundation for Norwegian Fiction and Non-Fiction Literature abroad (NORLA) and with financial support from the Research Council of Norway (NRC) and Akershus University College.

ISSN 1660-3443
ISBN 3-03910-348-2
US-ISBN 0-8204-7014-7


Hochfeldstrasse 32, Postfach 746, CH-3000 Bern 9, Switzerland
info@peterlang.com, www.peterlang.com, www.peterlang.net



Printed in Germany

Arne Ekeland: *Læring* 

*In memory of my mother Martha and my father Finn,*
*both of whom had experience as apprentices,*
*and for the apprentices and colleagues*
*in the vocational pedagogical sector*
*who have taught me to pose new questions*
*about the learning relationship between hand and mind.*

# Table of Contents

CHAPTER 5



*PART TWO*
*Gender and Skills in Vocational Education*

CHAPTER 6



CHAPTER 7

# Preface

In this book, I present a critique of existing models of vocational education, which are education preparing young people to participate in the present-day manual labour market. I then proceed to outline and advocate a workshop-focused pedagogical model for the future. This model draws upon my years of experience derived both from working in vocational education and from teaching vocational teachers to do research in the field of vocational education.

I worked for eighteen years as a welfare officer, counsellor, and lecturer at vocational schools in Oslo in relation to the crafts and industry vocational sector. Later I was appointed professor of vocational pedagogy in the Department of Vocational Teacher Training, University College of Akershus, Norway. For the past fifteen years, I have taught vocational pedagogy to students working on their thesis-based higher degrees. These students are vocational school teachers employed in upper secondary schools all over Norway. It has been a particularly rich and instructive experience for me to work with vocational teachers as they engage in research and begin to develop comparative and reflective knowledge in their various vocational specialties within the field of Norwegian education, and it is also a foundation for my knowledge of the development in upper secondary education during the latest reforms.

I have divided the book into three parts: In Part 1, I reflect upon the changes in upper secondary education in Norway in a historical and sociological perspective. I also discuss the educational changes in upper secondary education in Norway currently known as Reform 94. In Part 2, I focus on gender, which has its own history in modern vocational education research. In Part 3, I describe and analyse my use of workshop pedagogy in teaching at a university college and sum up my argument as to the practical and theoretical qualities of this method of pedagogy.

There is what we might call a red thread running through the book. The central issues here are the gender question in vocational education, the development of vocational schools for the crafts and industry sector, the relationship between vocational and general education, and the interface between very different learning styles – between those who learn from practical vocational instruction and through apprenticeship, and those who learn in the classroom. Workshop learning, as a promise of fruitful alternative pedagogies, is at the core of my arguments; moreover, it is addressed more fully in the final chapters, regarding the future of education.

My international contacts with friends and colleagues have had a significant effect on my work. To be able to compare the educational developments in one's own country with those in other lands contributes much to the understanding of both general and particular trends in the history and development of the vocational fields. I have long had research relationships with scholars and scientists abroad, especially at the Universities of Toronto in Canada, Joensuu and Tampere in Finland, and Adelaide in Australia. The 'journeyman wanderings' have been essential for my increased understanding of the wider field of vocational pedagogy. Colleagues in the research network 'Vocational Education and Culture Research Network', together with their annual conferences on vocational education, have been an additional source of great inspiration. In addition, critical scientific perspectives from the field of women's studies have allowed me to understand more about the distance between educational research and the everyday situation of vocational students and apprentices. Here I want in particular to thank Dorothy Smith and Hildur Ve.

I hope this book can contribute to a deeper interest in, and understanding of, both the unity and diversity of the vocational fields. Now, more than ever before, this general field has come to the fore in terms of research into education and learning. Nowadays, the relationship between education and working life is being discussed to a higher degree than ever before, both nationally and internationally. Vocational education is in focus, both in Leonardo da Vinci Projects across Europe and in international conferences. Vocational pedagogy is placing new pedagogical problems on the agenda, and is challenging the hegemony of the classroom-oriented school.

Every institutional system has its own building period, its period of consolidation and stability, and its period of decline. Perhaps we could say that learning, purely in relation to the school, has enjoyed its period of greatness during the last thirty years. Once again, new questions are being posed and new concepts are arising. I expect questions are always being posed and concepts are always arising. I just want to indicate that these are special, or that the occasion for them is special. You might say 'old questions are being raised again and old concepts are being revisited', or one might say that 'fresh' concepts or questions are being put forward in education fields as diverse as medicine, nursing, and the caring sector in general, or in trades in the crafts and industry sector. Concepts like 'master teacher', 'journeyman' and 'apprentice' are central in this connection. These concepts give rise to fundamental questions in the debate about teaching and learning.

There are many I would like to thank. First, the Norsk Faglitterær Forfatter-og Oversetterforening (The Norwegian Non-Fiction Writers and Translators Union) for economic support in the writing, the National Research Council of Norway, and NORLA (Association for Norwegian Literature Abroad, Fiction and Non-Fiction) for supporting the work of translating the book into English. Second, the degree students from Akershus University College who wrote their master's theses in vocational pedagogy have given me great insights and inspiration. I have also received the greatest of help and support from the librarians of the Department of Vocational Teacher Training, University College of Akershus, and I offer thanks to Peter Kell, Richard Lakes, and Martha Roldan who have given me constructive criticism concerning the English version of the book.

The help from Asgeir N. Portaas-Jore and Eva Andresen in the typesetting and indexing process has been invaluable. I thank Richard Daly, Bibbi Lee, and Charles Simonds for inspiration and stimulating discussions – the kind that lead one into new and exciting interior monologues – and Jeanette and Barry Scott, Wolfgang and Frigga Haug for peaceful places to work, and Will Lawson for his editing assistance.

Liv Mjelde

# Part One

# The Only Constant is Change: On the Development and Contradictions in Norwegian Vocational Education

CHAPTER 1

# Work, Learning, and Vocational Education

In the upper secondary school system in Norway over recent decades, the programmes of study for the vocations have undergone great changes and have been exposed to a succession of ideas. Back in 1965, the Schools Commission determined that vocational schools and gymnasia should be integrated into one system, and that all vocational education should be undertaken at school. The view then was that vocational education for the crafts and industry sector should be detached from ongoing developments in working life. However, in the wake of *Reform 94*, the term commonly applied to Norway's recent reforms in education, working life as a learning arena is once again central to vocational training and education. The main model for vocational education under *Reform 94* in upper secondary education (regarding 16-to-19-year-olds) is two years spent in school followed by an apprenticeship of up to two years in a trade.[1]

The *White Paper 33* (1992) laid the groundwork for the present reforms of upper secondary education in Norway. In the introduction to this White Paper we find that

> Teaching has been cast in two great traditions which both arise from the way the instruction of the young was organized during the Middle Ages. On one hand, in the guild system, education for working life took place within working life. The guilds developed both a specialization through the division of labour into crafts and a grading system of craft skills expressed in apprentice, journeyman and master levels. The other tradition also directed education into specialized functions, but this was considerably more theoretical and took place in distinct institutions: schools. A school was a liturgical group intended to serve the offering of prayers and masses. (p. 1)

1 Laws on educational matters in Norway are ratified by the parliament. The legal groundwork for Reform 94 was presented in Parliament in 1992 and came into effect in the autumn 1994. That is why it is called Reform 94.

These two traditions can be clearly observed both in the development of the public school system of Norway and in the vocational fields of study: learning in workshops and learning in classrooms. On the whole we have both types of teachers working side by side in vocational education, teachers trained as carpenters, mechanics, home economists and teachers trained in universities.

Characteristic of the school systems of Scandinavia in the post-war era is the quantitative expansion of public schooling and the professed aim of eliminating the class contradictions in society through the system of education. These are problems that have been part of the educational agenda all over the world (Hargreaves 1982, Livingstone 1987).

The only constant in the development of the educational system in Norway is reform. Contradictions between the two traditions have been at the core of the reforms during the past forty years. The constant need for reforms shows how complex these questions are. The reforms in vocational education for crafts and industry, the merchant navy and seamanship and the health and care sectors form the core of this book.

When I began my work in this field thirty years ago there were, in the world of related science and scholarship, few if any voices to listen to. The vocational trades were not on the pedagogical agenda. There was little research to be found in Norway and absolutely no systematic presentation of vocational learning or of the history and development of the vocational system. In 1973, Tore Lindbekk, professor of sociology, said that vocational school students and apprentices were a blank spot on the map of sociological research into schooling. Textbooks in pedagogy and the history of pedagogical theory presented their themes as though vocational students and apprentices did not exist. This has changed in recent years. Research that charted and evaluated educational changes following Reform 94 placed the vocational field and the apprenticeship tradition on the public agenda, and there is now research into vocational courses of study.

In pedagogy, we are beginning to see the development of an understanding that the field exists, but at the same time, we see this field contributing to the problematic on learning in general. The concepts 'vocational didactics' and 'vocational pedagogy' are important in this connection. The concept 'vocational education' is linked to the development of the manual labour market in the industrial era with roots in feudal craft traditions; the concept 'profession' is linked to academically trained work. Those in vocations and professions are supposed to do specialised work, and make use of specialised crafts and a specialized knowledge base in carrying out their work, in return for certain advantages. In both traditions, whether it is the hairdresser or the medical doctor, society awards the incumbent a monopoly in these specialised tasks. This social confirmation is derived from political decisions and acts of parliament. Both traditions face new pedagogical demands. Now a new concept, 'the pedagogy of professions' has entered the academic world.

## New Concepts: The Pedagogy of Professions, Vocational Didactics, and Vocational Pedagogy

The foundation of professional pedagogy took place in the universities of the Middle Ages, the institutions that created the fields of law, medicine, and the clergy (Henriksson 2001). In Norway, the study of professions as a field of research has a tradition to it in political science and sociology, but in terms of pedagogical questions, it has only been realized in recent years. Vocational pedagogy and the pedagogy of professions are concepts we also recognize from parliamentary white papers on educational reforms (NOU 1996, 22). The core of these reforms is the relationship between workshop learning and learning from the classroom and the lectern – between, on one hand, vocational fields, vocational theory, and general subjects in secondary education, and on the other, learning in practical situations in working life, whether this involves engineering, medical, or vocational fields of education. The concept of the pedagogy of professions seems to have become linked to the development of academic occupations, while the concept of vocational didactics seems to have developed basically within vocational education in the crafts and industry sector, the caring professions, the service sector, the development of vocational training in the secondary schools, and related apprenticeship schemes. Moreover, the concept occupation is used to refer to both categories. In the debates on the organization of teaching and learning, whether they refer to the pedagogy of the professions or to vocational pedagogy, we find not only similarities but also differences. Today, the concept of vocational didactics is related both to vocational education in the secondary school system and to higher education.

Work-based, or non-scholastic learning, learning as social practice, the master-apprentice traditions, and situated learning are now themes in the academic debate about teaching and learning both in Scandinavia and in many other places (Billett 2000; Boud&Symes 2000; Coy 1989; Daly&Mjelde 2000; Engestrøm 1986, Grosjean 2001; Harris et al. 1999; Kvale 1993; Lave&Wenger 1991; Nielsen& Kvale 1999; Wenger 1998). At least in Scandinavia, however, it seems that there is little linkage between the learning traditions in vocational education for crafts and industry and the academic debate on activity theory and the master-apprentice tradition. This is despite the fact that the master-apprentice system, and learning through social practice, is conspicuous in the everyday life of vocational school students and apprentices, whether this is at a workshop in the vocational course of studies, at the workplace where apprentices are located, or in adult education. It seems as though these two worlds belong to two entirely different physical and semantic universes without any dialogue occurring between them (see also Kvale 1993). Ole Johnny Olsen (2001) has addressed this in a study in which he compares the field of vocational pedagogy in Germany with the situation in Norway. He points out that the scientific field in Norway is more or less non-existent, while in Germany it has strong traditions with many participating in the vocational pedagogical debate.

The form of training within the crafts and industry sector in Scandinavia has been strongly criticized. The master-apprenticeship system has been portrayed as narrow and obsolete. The labour movement has disassociated itself from the apprenticeship schemes on the basis that apprentices can be exploited as cheap sources of labour (Isachsen 2000; Kvale 1993; Mjelde 1993; 1997a). I am not going to take up this issue here. What I want to do instead is investigate whether or not we can find a germ within this pedagogical model – taken from the workshops in vocational education for the crafts and industry sector, as it developed at school and in working life during the twentieth century – a seed that might give rise to a future education system. What I have in mind is an educational system in which the contradictions between the work of the hand and the work of the mind no longer exist, and in which the problems of learning, motivation, and meaning at school are solved.

## Learning Traditions in Vocational Education: Workshop Learning

Workshop learning in vocational education, whether in the kitchen, the mechanical workshop, the spinning and weaving floor, the hospital ward, or the operating room, places fundamental emphasis on learning through activity and collaboration. Learning through practice and experience – by trying and failing and through action – is the basis of true knowledge. Even in 'the realm of pure ideas', whether it be through the activity of writing or of teaching, one learns best when one is involved in activity (Applebaum 1992). We recognize this form of learning from the master-apprenticeship model of vocational education. Sissel Isachsen says that what is positive about master-apprenticeship learning is that it has transcended any contradiction between theory and practice by basing learning on practice in a natural environment (2000, 39).

Here, Isachsen is pointing to something that one observes very clearly in the development of any school-based vocational education, or in other words, any practice-based learning in the school workshops. This also applies to vocational theory, which is taught in school workshops and in classrooms, as well as to the general subjects, which have been insulated from the practical and vocational theory components of the course of studies and taught in separate classrooms. (It is normal practice to combine students from two different vocations for the classroom hours in the general subjects.) In the everyday language that has arisen with the development of vocational education at school, the school workshop learning is usually referred to as 'practice' and the general subjects as 'theory'. However this interpretation leads to a lack of understanding of the special features of the vocational pedagogical traditions. The specific learning traditions based on one's own activity, on the work of the hand in the workshop traditions, is unique to vocational pedagogy. Indeed it is crystal clear, and it must be stressed, that all work of the hand is based on mental activity. On the other hand however, this does not in the least mean that the theory concept is anything other than a generalizing of 'practical knowledge combined together and made systematic'.[2]

The activity of learning at the workplace is based upon a development in which practical knowledge has been assembled and systematized over thousands of years, and in which learning takes place through the processes of one's own activities as well as from interacting and cooperating with others. We find a special form of knowledge in vocational education within the school system, a meeting between the two unlike epistemological traditions – on one hand, that which is based on practice, and on the other, the academic tradition. The practical epistemology finds one in a workplace in working clothes, while when submitted to theoretical instruction; one is seated in a classroom in 'fine' clothes. Claude Grignon (1971) is one of the few who has undertaken empirical research into vocational education in France. He describes these contradictions in relation to

2 We often find this dichotomy in scientific discourse. José Luiz Ramirez (1998, 81) points out that talking about practice and theory as two different activities that exclude one another is an assumption that has invaded our culture and created a chronic illness in the realm of understanding. Former Norwegian Minister of Education Gudmund Hernes, who is also a sociologist, is fond of using the statement 'nothing is so practical as a good theory' without ever going into what this means (Hernes 2001, 114; see also Daly&Mjelde 2000, Sohn-Rethel 1978).

the society's common system of values. His main point is that vocational education at school reveals a projection of 'the established order' and a concretization of those mental structures through which individuals reflect on the relationship between different learning processes, intellectual and manual labour, and theory and practice. Contradictions and rivalries between workshop and classroom as arenas of learning, and between vocational teachers and general teachers, are significant in vocational education. In practice, there is at least one difference. The lesson times are longer in the vocational subjects – fifty-five minutes as opposed to forty-five minutes for the general subjects. This also reflects social organization in general and has much to do with the traditions and predominant values in society. One aspect of these traditions of evaluation is the way that academic education is awarded higher value than vocational education.

## Conflicts between Different Learning Traditions

The conflicts between different learning traditions have been important in all educational reforms right from the beginning of the nineteenth century. The relationship between vocational education and general education, between vocational subjects, vocational theory and general subjects has been, and continues to be, a major question in the carrying out of Reform 94. How is a subject to be learned – in the workshop or in the classroom? How are we to integrate vocational and general subjects? In which ways can the general subjects be oriented toward the vocations and professions? What is to be learned in school and what in the course of working life?

There are great variations in how these problems are being solved within the Nordic countries. In Denmark, employers and employees early on entered an agreement on apprenticeship schemes such that the building of workshops within the infrastructure of the school system has been little developed. Sweden went in the opposite direction and did away with apprenticeship systems. There, all vocational education occurs within Gymnasieskolan, the grammar school system. Finland

and Norway have to greater degrees followed the German tradition of dual systems, a combination of learning at school and learning at the workplace.

How have vocational students, apprentices, and vocational teachers experienced the development of the educational society in recent decades? What experiences have they had? The most important basis for my reflections and social scientific investigative work in the vocational pedagogical/vocational didactical fields over the last thirty-year period is, first, the experiences of vocational students, apprentices and teachers, and their practical discoveries of learning in school and in working life, and second, my own practice and experience from having worked as a welfare officer, counsellor, and teacher in the Oslo vocational schools.[3]

## Learning from One's Own Experience at Vocational School

I was hired as welfare secretary for both vocational schools in Oslo in 1967: the old Elvebakken Vocational School and the new Sogn Vocational School. This was the first 'social' position in the vocational school sector in Norway. The two schools had a common administration. Elvebakken was the first vocational school for crafts and industry in Oslo, with roots dating back to 1921. The foundation stone for Sogn Vocational School was laid in 1952, and the thinking at that time was that the school would be 'the Eton of the crafts and industry sector'. The plan in the mind of then education minister

3 The concept of experience is central to general pedagogical theory, as well as in scientific theory. In the course of my search for research strategies that include both my own and others' experiences, I have found instruction in Dorothy Smith's idea of experience. She is concerned with a research strategy that begins with the everyday life of people – the everyday life of the researcher as well as of the research subjects. She calls this the person's experience of self and the world one lives in, where one is both a 'knowing subject' and a 'social object of research' (Smith 1987; Mjelde 1993, 247).

Hjelmtveit was that 'the practical schools should be elevated in the realm of public consciousness, and be set up in the place where they belong, side by side with the academic schools' (Mjelde 1975b).

From its inception, the vocational school at Sogn had an annual intake of 3,400 vocational students and apprentices in fifty different vocational fields. Most went either for one-year workshop training at school or entered an apprenticeship programme in which they attended the school one day each week; others came to school for a month or half a year during their apprenticeship. In the period between 1967 and 1985, fifty thousand youth went through this school. In the course of my work, I had contact with thousands of these students in relation to the problems they had with various aspects of life: family problems, school problems, conflicts between teachers and students, or decisions regarding their future placement in the labour market. What was the possibility of getting an apprenticeship placement after one year of school workshop learning? Could they take their journeyman certificate if they had not passed the general subjects such as Norwegian, mathematics, or physics?

In the 1960s, nine years of compulsory schooling came into full effect in Oslo and I began to encounter students who did not adapt to the new school system. Students' unhappiness was a problem in many secondary schools. As early as the school year 1967–68, the vocational schools were receiving applications from other secondary schools for transfers of students who were in their seventh, eighth, and ninth years of study. The inspector of schools for Oslo set up a commission in June 1969 which was to develop guidelines regarding requests for exemptions by students who felt unable to complete the compulsory nine years of schooling. The commission recommended vocational schooling as an alternative because it was seen as 'different and practically oriented' (Kokkersvold&Mjelde 1982).

This has created a paradox that has long preoccupied me: first, the compulsory school system alienates the student in terms of learning methods, and then when these same students can no longer keep their heads above water, it offers them a place in the vocational sector of the upper secondary school. It appears that educational authorities look on workshop learning as simply a remedial exercise for those who fall out of the academic side of education, rather than a valuable approach to learning in itself. Similarly, in prisons and psychiatric treatment centres the prisoners and clients are offered courses based upon the vocational pedagogical learning traditions. The school workshop is the most important learning arena in this tradition.

In the post-war era, the gymnasia expanded to an even greater extent than the vocational schools. Consequently, it was possible in most areas of Norway for a student to obtain a place in his or her local gymnasium in the 1970s. The competition for entry into the vocational schools, which has always been intense, became even more so. As early as 1967, the vocational schools in Oslo informally started to integrate drop-out students from the nine-year comprehensive school program into those trades that did not have excessive numbers of applicants. There is a great variety of trades in the vocational school system, some more popular than others. The competition for entering some of these trades is fierce. There could well be two hundred applicants for the twelve available positions, for example in the radio-electronic, aircraft mechanic, and photography classes. Back then, other trades, such as masonry, butchering, and baking, were not so popular. In some classes, such as mechanics and home economics, there were so many positions available that placement was easier. But popularity also swings with the cycles of the labour market. For example, the 'electro' line may have many applicants one year during the boom stage of the labour market, and few the next year as the economic cycle decelerates.

Integration of special needs students into the mainstream became a major theme in European educational programmes during the 1970s, and various laws concerning this were passed there. In 1973, the Oslo School Board adopted a decision to reserve two places in each class at vocational school for students having a history of social/medical problems. The decision was remarkable in the sense that it gave priority to the less able. This policy reversal was in marked contrast to the traditionally competitive educational system. In Norway the law concerning the integration of disabled youth into the school system was passed in Parliament in 1977 (Vislie 1982).[4] In the period between 1970 and 1990, hundreds of students were accepted into

4 It is also part of EU's educational Programme Leonardo da Vinci.

vocational education on the basis of special needs, and thus avoided the normal competition around securing a place at a school. I worked closely with these students. They were young people who had trouble with the nine-year compulsory school system, or who had come out of prison or psychiatric institutions.[5] As school learning was vigorously expanded, the number of such cases grew and grew. They had one thing in common: they all had problems with learning in school settings. For many, school was experienced as devoid of relevance and meaning, and this had caused a loss of faith and confidence in their own ability to learn anything.

## Research into the Vocational Sector

In 1975, the Social Department granted research funds to carry out an investigation of students taken in on the basis of special needs. In the research project entitled Social Client Treatment at Vocational School we followed a three-year cohort (between 1977 and 1979) of special needs students accepted into the vocational sector. The results of this investigation showed that 70 per cent of this cohort was either working or at school at the time they were interviewed. Another common feature was the fact that they had flourished and managed to learn when they were in the school workshops organized on a master-apprentice basis, and that they tended to drop out of the subjects in general education. The students said that they had 'come home' when they began at the vocational school, a reflection of their desire for more relevant and collaborative pedagogies. This is also a class question. Vocational education has been the educational route of the working class with strong working class traditions (Kokkersvold& Mjelde 1982; Mjelde 1987).

5 There was often a correlation between these categories. Those who came out of detention centres and psychiatric institutions had often experienced problems with the nine-year school (Stang 1975; Hammer, Ravndal&Vaglum 1985 Kvalsund, Myklebust, Båtevik&Steinsvik 1999; KUFD 1999).

These findings have preoccupied me for a very long time and also occupied a central place in my doctoral dissertation which dealt with the experiences of apprentices with regard to learning at school and learning at work (Mjelde 1993; 1994a&b; 1997a). I interviewed 1,617 apprentices in five cities in Norway between 1982 and 1984. I interviewed these apprentices at vocational school during the periods when they were taking the classroom component of their apprenticeship training. Eighty-nine per cent said they preferred to learn on the job rather than at school. This was equally applicable to the compulsory nine-year school and the vocational curricula in secondary school. They found school to be meaningless. During one period I was an 'apprentice' in an industrial firm with seventeen apprentices, and I also participated in a graphics apprentice class with eleven apprentices during two six-week periods. The apprentices in these situations all preferred to learn on the basis of working life.[6] This introduces the following questions: What was it in the learning situation at school that failed to satisfy the students and stopped or impeded their learning? Also, what was it about the workshop venues at vocational school and on-the-job learning that created good learning situations?

What did these results of the 1975 research project and my doctoral thesis really tell us? During the 1980s I was a guest and research fellow at the Ontario Institute for Studies in Education (OISE) in Toronto, Canada. There I collaborated with researchers oriented toward cross-disciplinary work on the question of learning at school as opposed to learning at work. We worked with labour market theory and the division between intellectual and manual labour as this had occurred with industrialization. I gained considerable inspiration from participating in this milieu, and the experience helped me to understand dilemmas in the development of vocational education. Thus, over the years, I have worked away at trying to understand 'learning' and make it more overt and visible within the vocational study programmes. I have tried to study vocational particularities as a

6 This result came as a surprise to me and it took me years to really understand the reasons for the preference for apprenticeship over school instruction. Recent research among apprentices in Denmark gives the same results.(Mjelde 1993, Nielsen&Kvale 2003)

discrete area of knowledge within educational research, an area central for posing questions about learning in general, as well as being particularly challenging and meaningful in the pedagogical sense.

Vocational pedagogical knowledge has its roots in the workshop tradition of the guild system and in school workshops that developed with industrialization and saw the growth of vocational education at school.[7] Historical perspectives of vocational education in the crafts and industry sector are essential for vocational education's own self-awareness, both as a scientific and scholarly discipline and as a field of pedagogical research (Schriewer&Harney 1999.) It is important to develop an understanding of this uniqueness within vocational education and how it distinguishes itself qualitatively from general pedagogical thinking. It is important to develop vocational pedagogy and vocational didactics as a field with its own area of knowledge

Of course I am not saying that general pedagogy has a uniform character. It is a field full of debate and contradictions. In recent years we have had a more fruitful debate about problems of learning and teaching than we have had for a long time. Conflicts between different traditions of science and between different views on learning are a particularly lively part of both pedagogy and psychology. In my own work, I have also described these contradictions in work-of-the-hand-oriented professions such as architecture, dentistry, medicine, and surgery (Mjelde 1993, 32). The Department of Vocational Teacher Training at Akershus University College has worked with these complex problems in teacher education for vocational teachers over many years and has come a long way in advancing a praxis for vocational pedagogy and vocational didactics. But the complexity in the field is revealed in the following statement by a vocational teacher I interviewed in the 1970s: 'We learn the practice at vocational school, and at the State Vocational College (SYH) we learn the foreign words

7 I have travelled extensively in Latin America and Africa. I have visited vocational schools for crafts and industry in virtually every country I have visited. They are almost carbon copies of one another, whether one is in Santiago de Chile, Buenos Aires, Dar es Salaam, Lusaka, or Gjøvik in Norway. Argentina and Chile, by the way, had developed their school-based vocational education before we in Norway got our first workshop schools for crafts and industry (see Mjelde 1986).

and expressions'. Much pioneering work has been done in this field by colleagues in the Department of Vocational Teacher Training. The 1976 book by Per Drevvatne and Bjørg Johnsen was a milestone with regard to the systematization of project-based teaching (see also Drevvatne's doctoral thesis 1983). As I have mentioned, in more recent years as well, professional pedagogy and problem-based learning have been central concepts in connection with this debate. Hilde Hiim and Else Hippe (2001) have made an important contribution to the field with their book *'Å utdanne profesjonelle yrkesutøvere'* (Educating Professional Vocational Practitioners). Their critical point of departure has grown out of an understanding of the contradictions within the fields of nursing education and vocational teacher training.

## Learning in Terms of Vocational Didactics

In vocational pedagogy, learning in the school workshops and learning at work are two sides of the same coin. Learning, rather than teaching, is central to the didactics of this field (see also Nilsson 2000). Learning in the school workshops is of course not identical with learning in actual working life. There are similarities and differences between them. The main similarity between the school workshops and working life is that one learns through one's own activity in a work situation and through interaction with others. The difference is that learning a vocation at school is always a simulation of an actual working situation. The school situation is a model of reality in which a slice of reality is recreated, independent of the working stress of time pressure and demands for increased productivity and profitability. It is distinguished by its concentration on one slice of work reality. The learning involves the close study of this slice and taking time for exercises to develop skills and proficiencies that will be needed in future work situations but which now are learned independent of any actual production demands. This has advantages and drawbacks that are worth examining more closely. However, we still have only limited research insights into what the drawbacks mean in terms of content for vocational education required for meeting tomorrow's demand for vocational competence (Mjelde&Tarrou 1992, 8).

Vocational pedagogy is marked by diversity and motion. Old established crafts vocations die out and new fields are created. The crafts of shoemaking and tailoring are out and the training of information technicians is in. Home economics is out and care worker apprenticeship is in. The only constant is change. Work processes and vocational fields change in league with technological developments. Information technology has changed work processes both in the various vocational fields and in the teaching processes for these fields. We now talk about the new knowledge society and the computer revolution. The diversity of working tools – each of which served its specific functions in earlier work processes – are now often produced with the help of the computer chip and its multitude of functions and applications. The consequences this has for the organization of learning processes in vocational fields and for the development of vocational knowledge is something we are only beginning to come to grips with. The vocational fields are different when it comes to work traditions and relations with working life and the labour market. Some vocations have traditions that date back to the guilds. New vocations have come to the fore with industrial production and with the more recent development of the service society. Today more and more vocations are being added to the statutes and regulations concerning vocational learning at the workplace. In the crafts and industry sector, in health and the caring professions, and in the aesthetic subjects, education is marked by diversity and complexity. Every vocation has its particularities, even though vocational education is built of the same material, with its starting point in a pedagogical model where one learns from practice to theory.

The gendered division of labour is also clearly evident in vocational education. Some fields are completely male dominated, others are female dominated, and some have mixed-gender recruitment. Speaking generally, we find that home economics and handicrafts have been developed for girls, while crafts, industry, agriculture, seamanship and fisheries have been for boys. In addition, within the crafts and industry vocational sector there have been specific male and female traditions within various vocations (Mjelde 1975c; 1984c). Among other themes, this is a topic I examined in the project entitled 'Apprenticeship Schemes from the Woman's Perspective' (1992). I have also studied the development of home economics teaching, which began in the 1890s, and with the changes in traditional women's education in vocational fields in secondary school over the last twenty years or so (see Chapter 6). I have examined this in the context of changes in the labour market and family policy – themes which are also important in women's studies and gender research, but not often explored.

## The Chapters in this Book

Here, in Chapter 1, I have presented an overview of the contents of the book, outlined the problems indigenous to this field and my own engagement in these problems. In Chapter 2, I reflect upon educational changes in Norway that are currently known as Reform 94. I discuss the changes in the course of studies in vocational education. In Chapter 3 the apprentices express their experiences of learning at school and learning at work. Chapter 4 presents the thinking of Lev Vygotsky and John Dewey about learning, both from the perspective of human development and in terms of learning/teaching. This is discussed in relation to vocational students' and apprentices' learning experiences and the master-apprentice traditions in vocational education. Chapter 5 raises new questions in relation to Norway's Reform 94 and the central role of working life as an arena of learning. Chapters 6, 7 and 8 chronicle one of the major traditions in the development of vocational education in the school system; namely, gender-specific training for home economics and the caring professions. These have been, and continue to be, an educational sector dominated by women. Chapter 6 presents a social history of two of Norway's pioneer home economics teachers who led to the breakthrough whereby their field became a course of studies in the school system. Chapter 7 deals with the special gender patterns that have been part of the development of vocational education in the school system, together with the changes and the new challenges that have arisen with Reform 94. Chapter 8 takes up the debate about the participation of women in the vocationally skilled, semiskilled and unskilled manual labour market with industrial development. This is based largely on my own research on the changing division of labour and gender in the graphics industry.

In Part Three, Chapter 9 and 10 I discuss the magic of workshop learning and the education of the future. In Chapter 9 I build on my experiences in teaching vocational teachers to do scientific work towards a master's thesis in vocational pedagogy. Finally, Chapter 10 discusses the contradictions and dilemmas and raises questions facing the tradition of workshop pedagogy in our rapidly changing world and the promise it gives for the future.

Figure 1: Vocational learning in the 1970s and 1980s: here, an electrical workshop.

CHAPTER 2

# Reform 94: Was the Way Forward the Way Back?

Reform 94 is primarily a reform of vocational studies. The relationships in secondary education between education and work, learning in school and learning at work, and vocational education and general education are central aspects of Reform 94. The Apprenticeship Act, which many people thought was about to disappear, is once again of vital importance[8]. During the optimistic boom era of the 1960s, political intentions seemed to lean towards abolishing the Apprenticeship Act in favour of incorporating all vocational education into the school system, and at the same time, integrating vocational schools and grammar schools under the same legal umbrella. Reiulf Steen, the leader of the Committee on Schools of 1965 – concerned with the integration of vocational and grammar schools – and Gunnar Berge, who himself had been a shipyard mechanic's apprentice, both regarded the apprenticeship agreement as a system of exploitation[9]. Apprentices were seen as providing cheap labour power. There were also ideas afoot at the time about removing the realities of work life from the new developments in schooling. School was to be independent of the demands of society at large. On March 20, 1969,

8 The *Apprenticeship Act* was passed in Parliament in 1950, and revised on several occasions. Norway's school system has until now been mainly public: few private schools exist. It is a three-level system consisting of, (1) primary school comprising a ten-year comprehensive education (ages 6–16); (2) secondary education comprising different streams, vocational and academic (ages 16–19); and (3) higher education in universities and colleges.

9 I met Reiulf Steen and Gunnar Berge in connection with educational policy where these arguments were used in relation to the future of vocational education at the end of the 1960s and the beginning of the 1970s. (Both were prominent leaders in the Labour Party. Gunnar Berge later became President of the Nobel Committee for the Peace Prize.) It was during this period that I worked actively to start an interest organization for vocational students and apprentices. This organization, YLI, came into being in 1970 (Mjelde 1975a).

during a vocational education conference in Oslo, AUF, the youth organization of the Labour Party, proclaimed: 'It is just as important to get rid of the *Apprenticeship Act* today as it was to get it set up in the 1930s.'

## Ideals and Realities: The Integration of Vocational Schools and the Gymnasium

In the *Act on Upper Secondary Education* of June 21, 1974, vocational schools and grammar schools were integrated under one common parliamentary act. The law went into effect on January 1, 1976. Vocational schools and grammar schools were renamed 'upper secondary schools'. One idea behind this integration was to construct new schools with vocational studies and the academic programme under the same roof. During this debate, it was suggested that all upper secondary schools should be called 'gymnasia', as they had been called in Sweden (gymnasieskolan). This was a debate that lasted for years. The Labour Party representative on the School Committee of 1965 favoured 'gymnasium', and in the early portion of the committee's deliberations this representative was joined by the non-socialist members. As protest from many quarters mounted, the situation changed. Many of the supporters of 'gymnasium' did not want the vocational schools to have the right to call themselves by the rather august name, gymnasium, and from the vocational school quarter the question arose: 'Isn't the name 'vocational school' fancy enough?' As a result, 'upper secondary school' became the compromise term. The principal purpose of the new law was to create an interim period during which co-ordination and amalgamation of the various school systems would take place. This meant a merger to establish a common structure or framework into which all school systems could fit or be accommodated (Telhaug 1975). The framework was to prepare and provide conditions for more general education subjects in the vocational school. The structure should be created with an eye to breaking down the sharp differences between general education and vocational education. The hope was that the secondary schools of the future would avoid a situation wherein young people, after finishing nine years of compulsory education, would have to choose between a general education and a vocational school. The School Committee of 1965 established the principle of access to a combination of general and vocational education. Courses and curricula were to be coordinated so that the transition from one form of education to another, or from one profession to another, could take place with as little loss of time as possible. A two-year basic education programme was established wherein the combination of general and vocational subjects was crucial. The goal was clearly to establish a unified school system for the purpose of eliminating the existing class structure.

On October 25, 1990, the secretary of what had been the School Committee of 1965 said, in a lecture to the School History Association on 'The Upper Secondary School and the Idea of a Unified School System': 'Laws and parliamentary decisions are one thing, but reality is something else, and certainly something more. Reforms and changes in society are processes and these processes are just as much a product of profound forces in society as political decisions.' He discussed how the old school system with its two or three parallel schools – commoner schools, upper-class schools, and the gymnasium – reflected class division in society and contributed to its perpetuation. The Norwegian political left used the reflection of class division in the old school system as their main justification for supporting a unified school system. The political right, on the other hand, fought to retain the old system and its class divisions. The School Committee secretary showed how these contradictions were alive and well during the committee's lively discussions in the 1960s (Østvold 1990, 9). The contradictions were many and complex in this debate over the unification of vocational schools and grammar schools, but nevertheless, the law went into effect on January 1, 1976, and the upper secondary schools thereafter had a common governing body, The Council on Upper Secondary Education.

## The Integration of the Governing Body: The Council on Upper Secondary Education

In the 1970s, one of the issues in the ongoing debate was the question of the structure of the governing body of the new school system. The dismantling of the Vocational Education Council attracted particular attention (Mjelde 1975b). Until January 1, 1976, the vocational schools of the crafts and industry sector, from the *Vocational School Act of 1940*, came under the *Apprenticeship Act of 1950*. The Vocational Education Council was established by the Ministry of Education and Church Affairs in 1937 and was the originator of the proposed *Vocational School Act of 1940*.[10] The council represented Labour and Capital, both of which influenced the content and development of the vocational school sector. In organizational terms, the new aspect of the *Act on Upper Secondary Education* (of 1974) was that after January 1, 1976, the vocational fields of study were now governed by the Council on Upper Secondary Education, and Labour and Capital lost their influence on the development of vocational fields of study in the school system. This created one organizational structure for the apprenticeship system in work life and another organizational structure for vocational training in the upper secondary school system. The debate during recent decades about vocational education has been marked by contradictions among the members of the Council, between the representatives of Labour and Capital and the representatives of the scholastic traditions. The conflicts manifested themselves in the relationship between the Council for Vocational Training in Working Life (RFA), and the Council for Secondary Learning (RVO). RFA dealt with learning on the job, that is, with the apprenticeship schemes, and RVO stood for the development of educational facilities and subject planning for the vocational programmes of study. These efforts towards integration must be seen in light of the fact that school reforms also had a more

10 The act was not enacted till 1945 due to the occupation by the Germans from 7th of April 1940 till May 8th 1945 during the Second World War. The parliament did not function in this period.

'noble' purpose. School reformers regarded the Act on Upper Secondary Education as an effort towards a unified school system that would provide equal opportunities for all. Supporters of the act believed everyone should have the right to equal education regardless of gender, class background, and place of birth, and that the integration of vocational schools and the grammar school was integral to implementing equality.

## The New Upper Secondary School: Different Traditions Meet

The 'old' schools, which in 1976 became the new upper secondary schools, each had its unique traditions. The three-year gymnasium was a theory-based school for the select few; it had university-educated teaching personnel who prepared the students for higher education at the universities and colleges, and for academic positions in society. Vocational education for crafts and industry, with development of school-based learning in the form of workshop training schools and apprenticeship schools prepared for the manual labour market. The school of domestic science and household courses in the vocational schools also had a practical orientation linked to the solid traditions of rural needs and culture: well-behaved industrious students, confident teachers and leaders. The domestic handicraft school was also rooted in rural culture and designed to safeguard rural aesthetic values. The school for practical nurses, on the other hand, grew out of the developments in the health care sector in the 1970s. The nautical college-seamen's school was aimed at the merchant navy and seamanship. The commercial school was rooted in the so-called bourgeois or non-Latin school, which was strongly influenced by the culture of commerce. Farm management education grew out of the traditions of nineteenth century 'good old Norwegian farming' (Bjørndal, cited in Sunde-Gran 1993, 70–71). Originally these schools were worlds apart.

There was a major gulf between the gymnasium, or grammar school, and the vocational school.

The old traditional gymnasium did not prepare for a profession; it prepared for a university education. It was the only three-year school. The other schools were directed toward a profession – commerce and office work, housewifery, mechanics, or seamanship. Most of the vocational fields in crafts and industry were one-year workshop schools, the basic-course schools as they were called in the 1970s, and they were part of the dual workshop/apprenticeship system[11]. In the 1970s however, certain kinds of vocational education took place in three-year schools. Tailors and dressmakers, dental technicians, and students of radio and electronics had school education all the way through to their journeyman certificates.

The School Committee of 1965 discussed the idea of the right to schooling and compulsory schooling for all. They rejected the idea of compulsory schooling beyond compulsory secondary school. But access to schooling for an additional three years was now proposed as an absolute right for everyone (Østvold 1990, 4) In line with this thinking, the School Committee of 1965 recommended that all vocational education should take place within the schools, without placing students in contact with any workplace (Kokkersvold&Mjelde 1982). The assumption of the 1960s that the Apprenticeship Act was on its last legs reflected a general move to reinforce formal schooling and educational systems and a belief in the importance of knowledge to economic growth. The fundamental assumption here was that students could best acquire knowledge in a formal school context rather than in a workplace or non-institutional setting.

11 The vocational education system has been subject to extensive 'name changes' over the past thirty years. There were, for example, the Vocational School of Crafts and Industry with school workshops, and also apprenticeship schools with fields of study like carpentry or home economics. After January 1976, these vocational streams were referred to by such terms as the basic carpentry course, or the higher electro course, in the upper secondary school.

## The Renaissance of the Apprenticeship Scheme

In spite of a transition period during which the vocational schools and the *Apprenticeship Act* were to be integrated and taken into the academic school system, the former system continued to live a life of its own (see also Engen 1992, 2). Vocational education for crafts and industry, and apprenticeship training pursued their established trajectories in conjunction with developments on the manual labour market, remaining, as before, dependent on economic trends within the various fields. To respond to this, *The Act on Education in Working Life* was amended and changed, whereupon it was adopted by Parliament on May 23, 1980. Young people continued to choose different paths after compulsory school. Vocational education continued to be the educational path of the working class. Approximately one half of the compulsory school cohort chose vocational fields of study. My research, The Apprenticeship Study 1982–1984, showed that of the 1,617 apprentices who were interviewed, 50 per cent had started their apprenticeship directly, without basic education courses in vocational fields of study in upper secondary school. Forty-five per cent had taken basic courses in vocational fields of study before they started their apprenticeships (Mjelde 1993).

In the 1980s, training within working life once again strengthened its position by relying upon the terms of the *Apprenticeship Act*. Additional subjects were included in the apprenticeship law and the number of apprenticeship contracts increased considerably (Mjelde 1993, 78). The State also contributed with financial support agreements for businesses that accepted apprentices, and politicians began to put the relationship between education and work on their agenda (Mjelde 1988b, 16). The minister of church and education, Einar Førde, said that the relationship between education and work would become the most important political school issue of the eighties (*Aftenposten*, September 3, 1980). Another minister of church and education, Tore Austad, spoke of the strengthening of the *Apprenticeship Act* as an excellent pedagogical opportunity (Håndverk og Industri No. 4, 1983). The *Apprenticeship Act* was quietly experiencing its renaissance. This development culminated in a royal commission report, 'The Road Ahead to Study – and Vocational Competence for All', and a policy document, 'Knowledge and Skill: On Certain Aspects of Secondary Education' (NOU 1991, 4), in which reforms to vocational studies in upper secondary education were the central issue.

These reforms in secondary education came into effect in the fall of 1994 (Reform 94). Labour and Capital were once again players in the arena of school politics. There were renewed efforts to co-ordinate learning in vocational fields in upper secondary school with learning through vocational training in work life. Twenty years after *The Act on Upper Secondary Education* took away the influence of Labour and Capital on the development of vocational education; they were now once again major players in the development of vocational education and the *Apprenticeship Act*. This reversal suggests that the road ahead became the road back.

## Special Features of Vocational Education

Vocational education in school has emerged with the development of industrialism. The core of this form of education is work or labour, and it is distinguished by its intimate connection with the development of the country's production activities. In the academic learning tradition, school and work life are separated. In vocational education, school and work are integrated in workshop practice. It has its own pedagogical model and its own work mode, which are qualitatively different from general academic pedagogy. The learning arena in the development of vocational schools has traditionally been practical work, workshops, and laboratories, and the teachers have been recruited from the manual labour market. Workshop-based vocations, industrial specializations, commercial and office jobs, the agricultural and maritime sectors, domestic handicrafts, and the home economics traditions have been at the core of Norwegian vocational education. But behind the general label of vocational education there are many different kinds of education. As explained above, my reflections on this subject are principally rooted in vocational schools for crafts and industry and in the home economics tradition.

## School-Based Learning Traditions in Crafts and Industry

The first school-based education for apprentices in Norway dates back to 1802[12]. A school for apprentices was established on Sundays. Here the apprentices were taught subjects suited to their practical training in the workplace, such as Norwegian, arithmetic, and technical drawing. The first vocational school in Kristiania[13] (Oslo), the Preparatory School for Iron and Metal Workers, was established in 1910 in conjunction with the upsurge in industrial development at that time. It provided practical work in its own school workshops and some basic education in free-hand drawing, technical drawing, and knowledge of materials. The preparatory school for tailors was established in 1912 and was organized for the needs of craftsmen. The Oslo Crafts and Industry Association set up an education committee in 1915. In the following years, preparatory schools were established for many trades: goldsmiths, tinsmiths and sheet metal workers, sausage-makers and butchers, smiths, carpenters, printers, and bookbinders. In 1921, these

12 This is a brief sketch of a complex development. A more complete version may be found in my doctoral thesis (Mjelde 1993, 100–126). I based my presentation on Eyolf Andersen's (1984) *Norsk yrkesopplæring 1890–1940*, a series of historical documents about vocational training, official statements, and conversations with Trygve Bratteli about vocational training and education during the period between the two world wars. Wilfred Wassenden (1999) has examined the history of mathematics in Norway's vocational education. A University of Bergen research group has contributed to the development of knowledge about the special history of vocational education. This is an important field to develop.

13 The Oslo/Åslo of late Viking times was renamed by the conquering Danes in the seventeenth century, in honour of their King Christian IV. The Danish spelling, Christiania, was changed to Norwegian spelling, Kristiania, during the nationalist movement of the late nineteenth century. In the 1920s the city changed back to its original Old Norse name, Oslo.

were united under a common administration with the name Christiania Trade and Preparatory Schools for Crafts and Industry.

In these schools, the school workshop was the learning centre, and there the students performed practical work. They practiced making things, such as hammers and screwdrivers in the iron and metal workshop, and dresses and suits in the tailor workshop. In other workshops they made sausages, and printed and bound books. All teaching took place in the workshops. Craft theory, industrial drawing, and knowledge of materials were taught in the workshop or an adjoining room. The elementary workshop school, as it was called in 1911, became the model for a number of such schools throughout the country. These were preparatory schools for apprentices, and students who had been through the workshop schools were awarded a shorter apprenticeship.

The development of vocational education for crafts and industry grew after the Second World War, in both school and working life. The school workshop was the central learning arena in vocational school, with craft theory and general theory as supplementary classes. The advent of the *Apprenticeship Act of 1950* caused an enormous increase in apprenticeship agreements in the industrial sector of the economy. Big industrial concerns accepted apprentices from either the vocational schools or the seven-year primary schools. A complex dual system consisting of an alternating system of education in school and in work life was also established. But there were big differences between the various fields. Many businesses remodelled and expanded their school facilities (Kornes 1990, Mjelde 1993).

During the education and work debates of the 1980s in Norway, much attention was paid to the German dual system. What was extraordinary about this public discourse was that the participants overlooked the similarities in vocational educational development between Germany and Norway. Walter Heinz, the German professor of vocational education, says that the German system is called 'dual' because it exhibits the following characteristics: (i) there is systematic alternation between learning in school and learning at work, (ii) time spent in school is paid for by the state, and time spent at work is paid for by the business, (iii) education is governed by law and the state; the employee and the employer share responsibility. The German system was more systematic and more regulated than the Norwegian system, but both systems were dual in the sense that there is an alternation between learning in school and learning at work. We find some of the same traits in Norwegian vocational education up to 1976 and after 1994 (see also Olsen 2001).

Vocational fields of study in the Norwegian upper secondary school and the *Apprenticeship Act* must be seen as an integrated whole. In the development of vocational education there have been four traditional categories:

- Six-month or one-year basic courses providing basic training in a craft or industry trade and qualifying the student for a contract with a certified workplace. The apprentice's period of instruction is shortened according to applicable rules concerning time completed in vocational school. Some trades require two years of school before an apprenticeship contract is possible.
- Three-year complete workshop schools. The students receive their complete training in their vocation, right up to their journeyman examination.
- Practical-theoretical apprenticeship schools. The apprentice attends school the equivalent of one day per week, in the evening or in blocks of time throughout the year, for classes in craft theory.
- Course-work of different kinds, beginning training classes, advanced training classes, and adult education classes.

In all categories you have a strong relationship between the trade taught in school and working life. In some of the trades that had three-year complete training in the vocational schools, the student was placed in work places for different periods of time.

Home economics was organized as a six-month or one-year course, and this eventually became compulsory for some types of education in the care-giving professions. The workshop as the most important learning arena for vocational education, and the relationship of the *Apprenticeship Act* to learning in work life, are central aspects of education today, just as they were a century ago (Mjelde 1975b; 1988b; 1993).

## The Vocational and the General Fields in the Development of Vocational Education within the School System

Vocational subjects (workshop learning and crafts theory), on the one hand, and general subjects, on the other, have their special history in the development of vocational education within the school system. As early as 1905, the question of the relationship between vocational subjects and general subjects was brought up in connection with the development of vocational education for crafts and industry in school settings. The Vocational School Committee of 1905, using the German work school pedagogue Georg Kerschensteiner's theories as a point of departure, maintained that civic education must also be provided in connection with work schools (Andersen 1984, 80; Mjelde 1993, 56). The Kristiania Crafts and Industry Association of 1907 stated: '[I]t will undoubtedly be of the greatest importance to our industry generally and to the different crafts in particular to raise the level of knowledge among crafts and industry workers' (Recommendations of 1906 (1907), 28).

In the early part of the century, industrialization and technological developments began to demand a higher degree of knowledge than customary labour had. It was also a period in which political struggles around workplaces were extensive, and political conflicts were sharp. Georg Kerschensteiner visited Norway around this time and emphasized the necessity for the school to educate the working class in depoliticized citizenship. In his opinion, young people's participation in trade unions and political parties was not a good education in citizenship. Education was regarded as an important factor on both fronts.

In 1919, the Ministry of Church and Education set up a committee with a mandate to examine the relationship between general education and vocational education (Andersen 1984, 80–101). An important Labour Party school policy advocate, Johan Gjøstein, was the committee chairman. Anna Rogstad and Anna Sethne, two well-known school policy advocates, were also on the committee along with three representatives from crafts and industry. The Committee of 1919 expressed new pedagogical ideas, but in the political and economic climate of those inter-war years, school development and apprentice education were not central political concerns.

An interesting aspect of the committee's recommendation is a repeat of the divisions between the school representatives and the crafts and industry representatives. The school representatives wanted to place trade schools and technical night schools under the administration of the public school system. This proposal met with strong opposition from the crafts and industry sector. The same contradictions have been present in the discussions in recent times.

One view that these questions led to, and which is interesting in this context, was that then, as now, a bridge was to be constructed to close the gap between vocational education and general education by including Norwegian language and civics/social studies, mathematics, and physics in vocational and preparatory schools (as they were then called). These ideas have been retained throughout the development of vocational education in schools.

In the period between the two world wars, the development of vocational and preparatory schools was modest (Mjelde 1993, 72). In 1935 there were only ten workshop schools in the country. Three years later the number had increased to twenty-eight, and by 1945 there were forty-two. The construction of vocational schools was discussed during this period as an element in the struggle against unemployment.[14]

14 Prime Minister Trygve Bratteli was deeply involved in these questions in the period between the wars. He had been a roofer's apprentice before becoming unemployed. During a conversation about vocational education, he said that the Labour Party was primarily concerned with vocational education as an element in the struggle against unemployment (see Bratteli 1946). My interview with Bratteli took place at the Storting (Parliament) on March 12, 1982 (personal notes in author's possession).

During the 1930s it became evident to many people that vocational education generally should be strengthened. In Parliament (Storting) in 1937, cabinet minister Hjelmtveit said, 'We have neglected to improve our vocational training and we have not taken care of that connection between our school system and our business community the way we should have.' A committee was formed to draft the Act on Crafts and Industry. In the Odelsting, where the act was debated and approved in 1940, the minister of church and education said, 'This Act will elevate practical schools and contribute to an increased general public awareness, and place them where they belong, side by side with academic schools.' This provides another perspective on the relationship between vocational and general education. The inclusion of general subjects in the vocational school was desired and considered necessary according to the ethic of social equality. These ideas and practices have been part of the development of the relationship between vocational fields and general education right up to the present, when the notions of social equality are being challenged by a marketplace 'free consumer choice' apparatus which threatens to displace the role of the state.

It was only in the period following World War II, after the *Act on Vocational Schools for Crafts and Industry* had taken effect in 1945, that general-education and university-educated teachers of academic subjects fully became part of vocational education. In 1946 there were forty-two workshop schools for crafts and industry. Practical work, vocational learning, and technical drawing constituted 70 per cent of the school week; 30 per cent was allotted to more general subjects (Wasenden 1997). In 1958–59, there were 69 vocational schools with 5,200 students. In 1971 the figures had risen to 105 schools with 35,846 students.[15] In this period, workshop and vocational streams were the central elements in the development of vocational education, while the extent of academic subjects also increased in relation to vocational education. On January 1, 1976, the vocational schools and

15 Sources: Storting White Paper No. 97 (1964, 65), 'On a country-wide plan to further construct vocational schools for crafts and industry, commerce and office work etc. for the period 1965-71'. NOU 1976, 10: *The Future of Vocational Education.*

the old gymnasiums integrated under one common law. But the systems continued in many ways to live their own lives independent of each other. The vocational schools were renamed, but the organization of learning in a complex combination between learning in workshops at vocational schools and out in the world of working life continued in the hundreds of different trades. The competition to get into vocational schools and apprenticeship was as strong as ever. The real changes within vocational education came first with Reform 94. The main pattern was now going to be two years in school and then two years in apprenticeship. A further topic of debate has centred on the relationship between breadth and specialization, which will say the relationship between vocational subjects and general subjects in the first two years. The entrance courses were reduced from 108 to 13 (see below, p: 57–58) and more general education is introduced in the first years and workshop learning was reduced from the autumn of 1994.

## After Reform 94: Now What?

Following the enactment of Reform 94, there has been an impoverishment of workshop learning and the vocational subject traditions. Ole Johnny Olsen (2001) points to how the brochure about the school system put out by the Ministry of Education and Research seems to diminish and exclude vocational education and the existence of the *Apprenticeship Act*, and to ignore its autonomous position. He shows that in this six-page information brochure on the new unified school, there is only one sentence dedicated to vocational education. He also shows the same tendencies on the administrative level. Specific vocational offices have been closed, such as the Council for Vocational Education in the Workplace and the offices of the various educational councils for each trade. This contributes to the weakening of the constructive learning arena in vocational education and runs counter to international tendencies where work-based learning and vocational learning traditions are central and used more and more in the post-compulsory years (see Chapter 5).

There have been many points of view about learning in school versus learning at work, practical versus academic education, and classroom versus workshop, and different views have emerged at different times. Many of the opinions about these contentious questions have different origins – school reformers, politicians, craft and industry leaders, and labour unions. All have particular motives and agendas for what they wish to be a part of the three components of vocational education. But there is a crisis today in the division of labour in society, and we have greater insight into what the educational community lacks. New questions are being asked, and we have a better understanding of the unproductive contradictions arising from these longstanding divisions (see Mjelde 1997, 331; Mjelde &Daly 2004).

## The Relationship between Practical Subjects and General Subjects in Vocational Education

Lennart Nilsson (1981b, 37) states that what characterizes the development of vocational education in school are that it has three components: practical (work technique), vocational theory, and general education. The practical component comprises teaching the techniques of practical work. The vocational, or craft, theory component has to do with teaching about materials used and how tools and machinery function. The general education component teaches general academic subjects such as Norwegian language and civics/social studies, history, foreign languages, mathematics, and subjects of a scientific nature such as physics, chemistry, and biology. The acquisition of knowledge in relation to these three components within the framework of 'professional knowledge' has been regarded differently by society at different times.[16] When vocational education was folded into the school system at the end of the crafts era and the beginning of the industrial era, vocational knowledge was transformed into school subjects and distributed as lectures and teaching.

Nilsson (1998) presents the following breakdown:

| Practical Component of Work Technique | Vocational Theoretical Component | Academic Component |
|---|---|---|
| Training in the use of tools and their function in actual work | Knowledge about materials, use of tools and equipment, technical drawing | Norwegian, civics, mathematics, physics, chemistry, etc., unrelated to vocation |

Table 1: The relation between practical and general subjects in vocational education

This shows clearly the social organization of the distinctive forms of knowledge we find in the development of vocational education within the school system. The learning arena for work technique has been the workshop and in the general subjects has been, and remains, the classroom.

Vocational theory has been taught in connection with practice in the workshop or in special classrooms. It has been different for different trades and at different times during the development of vocational education in school. Vocational theory is closely linked to each vocation's special content and development. Vocational theory provides knowledge about the materials, tools, and machinery used in the different trades. Technical drawing and reading blueprints are part of vocational theory. General subjects have been separated from the

16 I thank Lennart Nilsson for his constructive comments. In the Norwegian original I have kept the Swedish term *yrkeskunnande* because I have not found a good Norwegian equivalent. 'Vocational knowledge' is perhaps closest, but it lacks the internal dynamic implied in the Swedish *kunnande* (knowing). As I read it, this is linked to Vygotsky's understanding that *praxis* necessarily precedes *nomos* in terms of human ontological development (see also Bruner 1996, 152).

vocational part and have not been tied to any particular field. The introduction of general theory into vocational education provided positions for teachers with a university and college background in this type of school. Two different educational models meet here, the practical tradition and the 'book-learning' or academic tradition (see also Tarrou 1995; 1997).

## Two Different Ways of Organizing Learning[17]

We can gain another (and important) perspective by examining the two different ways of organizing learning that one sees clearly in vocational education.

According to the model shown in Figure 2 below, activity (practical work assignments from real life) is the crucial foundation for teaching and learning. You learn Norwegian, physics, and mathematics in relation to activity. This is illustrated by Mikkel Bongo (1998) in his master's degree work (Figures 2 and 3). Another way is to use each specific subject as a point of departure; here the subjects are taught by specialized teachers in a classroom (Figure 3).

17 Masters degree students' work is an important source of inspiration for coming to grips with these contradictions. The students document new knowledge in the field. Vocational education pedagogue Mikkel Bongo has been the principal of an integrated upper secondary school who daily encounters these problems, while also writing and documenting the vocational field (see Bongo 2001a).

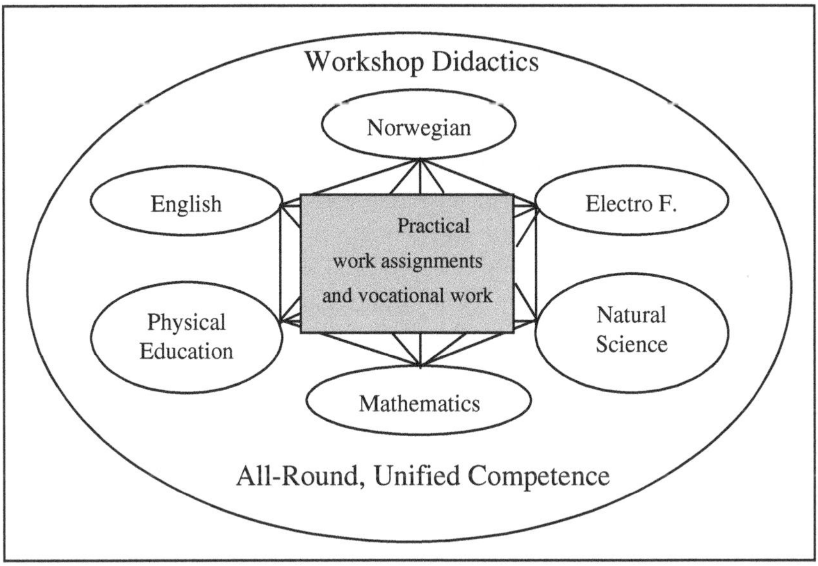


Figure 2: Workshop: Imagine what a load these people could lift if they worked together!

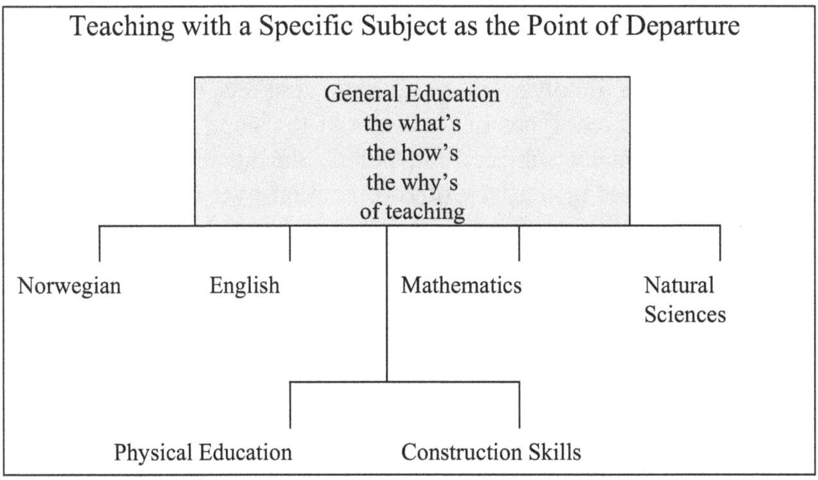


Figure 3: Classroom: Each teacher is solely responsible for him/herself and his/her students.

These figures illustrate two different models of organizing learning. In the first figure we have the workshop, founded on practical activity and a master-apprentice tradition. In vocational education this pedagogical model is linked to practical work tasks and to learning that takes place in cooperation with others. The second figure shows the characteristic aspects of the academic school model. Students arrive in the classroom for two hours of Norwegian, one hour of mathematics, and one hour of physics or biology. This learning tradition is characterized by lectures and teaching – a form of teaching in which the teacher sits at his/her desk at the front and faces a passive audience of students sitting in rows. Didactic thinking originates here in the logical structure of each subject, which along with the goals of the curriculum forms the basis for the planning, execution, and evaluation of teaching. Teaching in general education has been characterized by strict separation between the different subjects, although today there seems to be some conscious effort to integrate the programmes. These contradictions, which are so easily observed in the development of vocational education in the school system, have been crucial in all educational development.

The didactic model in current use involves a fragmented form of teaching. Eight different teachers may teach the basic courses in vocational subjects in the present-day upper secondary school. With so many people involved in one class, conflicts may easily arise between the different types of teachers. At the same time, the student must relate to many subjects and people during the same learning process. If there is also a lack of co-operation over content, teaching may easily become fragmented rather than integrated.

Mikkel Bongo (2001a) claims that this theme is especially prevalent since the introduction of the new curriculum for vocational training programmes following Reform 94. The introduction of the new curriculum brought into focus a clearer division between the vocational components of work technique and vocational theory on the one hand and general subjects on the other. In the 'old' curricula, the general subjects were described in the same curriculum along with the vocational subjects and were called vocationally-oriented general subjects. The new curriculum plans refer to vocational theory as 'general subjects'. As a result of this change, the teaching of general subjects – language and literature in particular – has been taken over by teachers with a background in fields other than vocational education. These are contradictory processes. Reform 94 has given rise to a deeper division between the vocational and general components of the new 'integrated' upper secondary school system. But on the other hand, we see that the problem area of integrating vocational and general subjects has come into focus more than ever before. New concepts about work-based learning and vocational didactics have emerged and are part of the general debate.

## The Road Forward to Higher Studies and Vocational Competence for All

The Blegen Committee's (NOU 1991) The Road Ahead to Study – and Vocational Competence for All made visible the problems of the vocational field sector in the upper secondary school. During the twenty-year period prior to 1994, most of the young people who started in vocational fields had few chances of obtaining a complete vocational education. A mere 11 per cent of the students in first-year courses enjoyed the opportunity of continuing their education, and only 3 per cent entered their third year. There was also great competition for placement in basic courses in many trades. In 1988, there were 550 applications for 90 places in graphics. Of these, 45 students entered secondary courses. The competition for apprenticeship positions was also great. The right to a three-year education for all young people between the ages of sixteen and nineteen, as suggested by the Steen Committee and including all students in vocational education fields, was an illusion.[18] Another problem for those who chose a vocational field at age sixteen was the fact that vocational

18 A lot of youngsters who entered vocational courses did never have a chance to complete their education. This is being questioned in European adult education currently and the concept of lifelong learning and new impacts on adult education is part of this critique (see Antikainen 2005).

education did not provide study competence, a controversial question also in the Blegen Committee recommendation.

The main points of the reform have been characterized as the reform of rights, structure, and content:

- All young people were given the legal right to a three-year upper secondary education.
- Vocational training in upper secondary school was to be coordinated with two years in school followed by two years in working life. The two years in working life were to include one year of training and one year of production.
- The number of basic courses was reduced from 109 to 13. The content of the basic courses was to be broad and general. Specialization related to the chosen vocation was to take place in continuation courses.
- Learning in school and learning at work were to be coordinated.

*Reform 94* has made visible the problems in the vocational fields and has put new questions on the agenda. The relationship between learning in school and learning in working life, between vocational and general academic teachers, between what learning constitutes in practical trades and what it constitutes in traditional general education, has taken on a new dimension. During the first year programme in vocational studies, the number of classroom hours in the academic portion of the programme has become higher than the number of hours devoted to vocational subjects. Workshop practice has been considerably reduced. The question arises as to the efficacy of traditional general education and the additional two years of classroom attendance before the students confront working life. Has it created bigger problems and more rejection of learning among those who did not like primary school and those who want vocational education and to begin to join the labour market and the working world at the age of sixteen?

The establishment of a ten-year compulsory school has brought a significant increase in the amount of discontent and drop-out problems among students (Sandven 1971; Mykletun 1975). Dropping out has also become an increasingly greater problem in vocational fields of study, a fact evident from follow-up research (Mjelde 1973; 1977; Hertaas 1990; Kvalsund, Myklebust, Båtevik& Steinsvik 1998; Mjåland 1994; Ulstrup-Engelsen&Ulvund 2000). On the other hand, the question of vocation education students having the right to full vocational education in school and working life has been placed on the agenda for the first time. Education for instructors and co-ordination between the learning of vocational trades in school and learning in working life are now part of public policy. How conditions are to be provided in order to make this happen is a complex issue within the many-faceted world of vocational trades, but the problems areas are more defined than ever.

To sum up: one of the main problems in the vocational fields of study is the relationship between workshop, vocational theory, and general subjects. How do we cover applied mathematics, physics, and chemistry in each vocation or each technical field? What about the subject of Norwegian language in vocational education (Berg 1999; Wasenden 2001)? In his doctoral work on the place of mathematics in the development of vocational education in the school system, Wilfred Wasenden (1999) shows that from 1912 to 1974, if we view all crafts and industry apprentices as a whole, mathematics as a subject has been of a rather general nature with respect to content. Analysis of mathematics in the apprenticeship curriculum in comparison to that of the old gymnasium shows that there are many similar aspects. In this instance, the counterpart to this mathematics teaching in the general education sector is mathematics in the vocational sector, where the teaching of the sciences is connected to the needs in the different trades.

In other work, Wasenden (1997) describes how the debates about these questions often have been dramatic and coloured by professional and ideological contradictions. He shows that in the period between 1974 and 1994 students in school workshops and apprentices could pursue vocational curricula in mathematics. But he also shows how it gets complicated when one tries to reach unambiguous criteria for fulfilling teaching requirements that ought to or must be viewed as directed either to the vocational or the general component of the course of studies. He points to the necessity of focusing on many facets of vocational education and the need for special training in theoretical subjects. This is one of the challenges of the content reform in Reform 94. I deal with these problems in the next chapter.

Figure 4: Vocational learning from the 1970s and 1980s. Here, a printing workshop.

CHAPTER 3

# What Do I Need Theory For? I'm Going to Be a Printer

## Learning at School and Learning at Work

The relationship between classroom and workshop learning in vocational studies is central to the reform process in secondary schools. There are those who maintain that one of the goals of *Reform 94* was to continue the process of integrating vocational and general education in relation to vocational curricula. The goal of the school reforms is to bring the two traditions together. The question is, how is one going to achieve this goal? The documents that have accompanied the reforms do not pose the difficult pedagogical questions that are implied here: How are workshop learning, vocational theory, and general theory to be integrated? Where is learning supposed to be conducted – in workshops or in classrooms? How should vocational and general teachers cooperate with regard to project-based learning? What kinds of learning models should be advanced in order to reach these goals – the pedagogy that has been spread through the workshop tradition in vocational training, or the pedagogy that developed with the grammar school classroom tradition?

The characteristics of vocational education are both unity and complexity. What the different trades have in common is the workshop tradition, learning from practice to theory. On the other hand, the field is enormously complex with more than two hundred different vocational trades listed in the legislation on vocational on-the-job training. This is a field that is constantly developing in tandem with technological changes, changes in work processes, and the demands of a constantly shifting labour market. This is the background for the reforms in the study programs for the vocations.

*Reform 94* has placed new questions on the agenda and brought the vocational curricula into focus in a new way. During the twenty-year period preceding *Reform 94,* there was enormous competition for places in the vocational programs on offer within the upper secondary school system. Only very few managed to secure for themselves an adequate education (Mjelde 1993). As mentioned before, the Blegen Committee showed that it was possible for only 11 per cent of students in basic vocational courses to continue for a second year at school, and only 3 per cent for a third year (NOU 1991, 4, 14). The competition for apprenticeship places was also great, and this in the face of an ideology that wanted to dismantle the apprenticeship system.[19]

During the 1990s, the apprenticeship system has enjoyed a renaissance and has spread to new fields and new vocations. At the same time however, the academic classroom requirements that precede apprenticeship have been lengthened. Many societies have considerable experience with the twelve-year academic classroom curriculum. One of its greatest problems is high drop-out rates. In the USA and Canada, both of which have had the twelve-year school system for a long time, 30 to 40 per cent of students drop out before completing high school. The drop-out rate from the vocational fields of study (oriented to the crafts and industry sector) in upper secondary schooling has also been an increasing problem in Norway – especially with the development and expansion of classroom-based vocational education – and this problem has not been solved with *Reform 94* (see also Bergli 1997, 21).

One of the contradictions that I will discuss here is learning in the work situation and learning at school viewed in relation to the new secondary school system, the system that has been developed over the last thirty years. Another contradiction that I will discuss is the relationship – or the lack thereof – between workshop learning and

19 Out of about twenty annual cohorts whose members began vocational courses of study over the last twenty-year period, many have not had the possibility of completing their education. A great number of them have entered and left labour market courses during this twenty-year period, and they have been very much affected by the upward and downward swings of the economic cycle, and are particularly prone to unemployment (see also Lien 1995; Magnussen 1995).

classroom learning within the vocational fields of study at secondary school. I intend to discuss contents and dilemmas within contemporary educational reforms – as these have emerged from my research over the last thirty years – about how vocational students and apprentices perceive their daily learning processes both in vocational school and at the workplace (Mjelde 1990a&b; 1993; 1994a&b; 1996a&b; 1997a&b). The Ministry of Education initiated 'follow-up research' in relation to the implementation of *Reform 94*. The Reform was subject to extensive evaluation in the first years after its implementation and I rely upon these evaluation reports in this account (Bergli 1995, 1997; Bergli&Frøyland 1995; Bjørnavold et al. 1995; Blichfeldt et al. 1996; KUF 1999; Monsen 1997; Olsen&Seljestad 1996).

## From Education for the Elite to Education for All

The Norwegian education system has developed at an explosive speed in recent decades. Forty years ago, education beyond the compulsory seven-year schooling was the domain of the elite. In 1956, only 16 per cent of an annual cohort of fourteen-year-olds had more than seven years of schooling. Eight per cent went to vocational school or found apprenticeships, and 8 per cent went on to either gymnasia or grammar schools. Today, almost 100 per cent complete the compulsory ten years of basic education and go on to attend secondary school. Fifty per cent begin vocational programs of study and 50 per cent take general higher education. Norway has had a quantitative expansion of the educational system at all levels.

At the same time there has been an integration of all the earlier types of schooling which formerly reflected the class divisions in society. The statute of 1959 replaced the old secondary modern and the grammar school with nine years of compulsory primary education. After January 1, 1976 the vocational schools and gymnasia were integrated under one law. The idea of equality was one of the expressed goals put forward by the Norwegian Labour Party

(Skinningsrud 1969; OT.PROP. 18, 7). A fundamental goal of this new statute was to bring about equality between practical and theoretical education (KUF 1982, 19). A second goal was to give equal opportunities to young people without regard to class background, geographical region, or gender. Research conducted in Scandinavia, as well as all over the Western World, has shown us how complex these questions are (Charlot 1987; Hargreaves 1982, Hernes&Knudsen 1976; Livingstone 1987; Kokkersvold&Mjelde 1982). We still have 'a reproduction of inequality' throughout the education system (Hernes 1974; Utdanningsspeilet, 2004). The division of curricula between vocational and general subjects is part of this complexity (see also Gaskell 1992; Mjelde 1993; Tanguy 1985).

Both general and vocational education programmes prepare youth for the labour market. However, traditional gymnasium education has a liberal academic content that does not refer directly to the labour market, but rather opens the way to university and college studies, and subsequently to a more prestigious labour market.[20] Over time, what distinguishes developments in the vocations is the actual stage of the economic cycle with respect to the manual labour market. This market swings rapidly and seemingly in an unpredictable manner, but recruits youngsters mainly into working-class positions in the craft industrial and service sector.

20 One of the more controversial political questions rose in the area of education in the past thirty years has been the creation of broader access to university and college programmes of study. In the 1970s, the Bjørnson Committee proposed building up nursing assistant qualifications to full nursing and medical doctor in a step-by step manner. One should be able to enter the academic studies at college and university level through vocational education. This proposal encountered strong protests from the professional unions and failed to get a parliamentary majority in 1975. One way of raising the professional prestige of women in the caring professions has been to demand grammar school graduation as an entry requirement. This has shut out youngsters with a vocational background, and consequently has been a controversial issue in the Blegen Committee's recommendations regarding the new reforms to the upper secondary school programme of 1994. The new socialist–green government of September 2005 has proposed to open University studies to graduates of vocational programmes, such as carpenters and mechanics and this has created protests from the directors of the universities and university-colleges.

Over the last thirty years, one of the main themes in the sociology of education has been 'the reproduction of inequality'. At the same time, in this debate the relationship between different learning traditions – academic education and vocational education – vis-à-vis the development of the school has been very little discussed. Was the integration of the old secondary modern and grammar school into the new nine-year comprehensive school in Norway in 1959 carried out according to the premises of the old Latin school? When the question of integration of the grammar schools and the vocational schools came up, anxieties were expressed that the same thing would happen, and that the vocational schools would lose their special pedagogical model based on workshop learning (Kokkersvold&Mjelde 1982).

Nevertheless, with regard to educational goals, the June 21, 1974 statute on continuing education was a great step forward for vocational students and apprentices. The statute about vocational schools for crafts and industry (March 1, 1940) had included a clear paragraph on its goals:

> Vocational schools for crafts and industry have as their goal to educate craftsmen and skilled workers, technicians and engineers, as well as other skilled personnel in relation to the demands that working life poses at any point in time

The corresponding paragraph on goals for the old gymnasium reads:

> Grammar schools and gymnasia are continuing general education schools. They are to contribute to the pupils' Christian, ethical, social, aesthetic and physical upbringing, give the pupils knowledge and develop their work skills and proficiencies. (Lov om gymnaset 1964)

Here we see great differences in how students should be socialized for different class positions in society. In distinction to the grammar school, the students of the vocational school and the apprentices required no Christianity, ethics, or aesthetics. They were to be educated in accordance with the demands made by the labour market at any one point in time.

Then came the version set out in the statute of June 21, 1974:

- The secondary school shall prepare the students for work and for life in society, provide a basis for further education and help students in their personal development.
- The secondary school shall contribute to the development of knowledge about and understanding of basic Christian values, our national cultural heritage, the democratic ideas, and scientific methods of working and thinking.
- The upper secondary school shall uphold human equality and equal opportunity, freedom of thought and tolerance, ecological understanding and international joint responsibility.

According to the law regarding secondary education, all students should be trained in scientific methods of thinking and working, should be prepared to participate in work and social life, and should be helped in their personal development, and school should lay the basis for further education.

Yet the contradictions in school and society are not solved by means of a paragraph of intent. The contradictions between the workshop subjects and the field of general education, between vocational teachers and general academic teachers, remain very much alive. Vocational and academic curricula recruit personnel from different sectors of the labour market. Vocational teachers have a double practice-oriented background in the execution of the subject they teach (Mjelde&Hammer 1979; Mjelde&Tarrou 1992; Tarrou 1988; 1995). Most frequently they have the typical training of vocational workers and have experienced the manual labour market. Those who teach in the general education sector most frequently have a background of academic education behind them and have spent their working lives within the education system. Vocational education is directly linked to the economic cycles in the manual labour market. Traditional gender divisions in the various vocations are also a constant feature of vocational education and reflect the manual labour market and society. We find the boys in the 'hard fields' and the girls in the caring sector and aesthetic vocations (Mjelde 1975b&c; 1984c; 1992).

There are basic contradictions in society that one finds reflected in the growth and development of schooling and which have their roots in the division of labour that has developed with industrialization. There are contradictions between so-called *practical* knowledge and *theoretical* knowledge, the *work of the hand* and the *work of the mind*, *manual labour* and *intellectual labour,* general and academic learning traditions, and inductive and deductive methods of thinking.[21] In the curricula of the vocational sector these contradictions manifest themselves very clearly in the division between workshop and classroom learning. These learning traditions are described here as 'ideal' in their depiction of the practical and the academic worlds. One finds the same contradictions in the study of medicine, dentistry, nursing, and architecture, subjects that are all closely related to the work of the hand (see the chapter 'School Is a Lousy Place To Learn In' in Howard Becker 1986). These paired concepts also describe society's prevailing values. In the development of the school system in general, and of vocational education in particular, we certainly find these contradictions. They have also led to the theoretical impoverishment of vocational education in the course of the last century (Jackson 1992).

The question of the contradictions between vocational fields and academic subjects is at a higher level in the education debate than it has ever been. At the same time, there is little evidence of insight into the realities of these contradictions (see also Nielsen&Kvale 1999).

21 The popular college tradition (folkhøgskole tradisjonen) in Scandinavia also has its origins in these contradictions. Grundtvig's ideas about the division between the work of the hand and that of the mind are at the foundation of the development of more holistic arenas of learning such as we find in the popular colleges or 'folkehøgskolene'.

## How the Apprentices Experience the Dilemmas

In the course of conducting a large research project on work and learning, I interviewed 1,617 apprentices in five Norwegian cities. I also participated in, and observed, an apprenticeship class in a large mechanical firm, and an apprenticeship class in graphics within the vocational curriculum (Mjelde 1990a&b; 1993; 1994a&b; 1996a&b). Out of the 1,617 apprentices, 1,438 or 89 per cent preferred learning in the work situation to learning at school.

The weight of 'practical work', of 'doing something real', of 'being paid for it' and 'good work mates' were the expressions used by apprentices about their contrasting experiences at work and school. They considered school to be far away in a world divorced from real life. Testimonies like the following were common:

- I think it's totally meaningless to go to school. When you are working you have responsibility. Economically it's better than school. It's more responsible and more interesting. (Welding apprentice). This apprentice stressed that he felt school was without meaning, and to have a feeling of responsibility was important to him.
- School gives you no clue about the actual reality of work and how things develop. School wears you down with all its theoretical subjects. (Graphics apprentice)
- Working life gives you a much better and more natural education. (Mechanic apprentice)
- What's most important is practice at the work place. Much of the theory is really all right, but what you can't learn at school is how to work independently. I have always liked to work. The neighbours call me a workaholic. (Carpentry apprentice)
- I think there's too much schooling. I think in my field it's best to work among your clients, not just among a bunch of books. (Hairdressing apprentice)

Even though many apprentices were also critical of their experiences as apprentices, they felt that in their apprenticeships they were more useful, freer, part of the adult world, and part of the real working world (Mjelde 1993, 90–94, 101–104; see also Olsen&Seljestad 1996, 117–32).

Eighty-nine per cent of the apprentices preferred learning in the work place over learning at school, that is, compulsory schooling or the basic vocational training program. One result of the research survey was that the 45 per cent of apprentices who had taken the basic vocational training course before they began their apprenticeships were critical of the content of the basic course. They claimed it was too far removed from 'real life'. In the field of vocational education, one of the contradictions between learning at school and learning at work is the fact that technological developments in recent years in these fields occur very quickly, and the cost of machines and equipment is great. The schools are not economically equipped to buy the latest equipment. Here are some comments from apprentices in the graphics class:

- School just can't give you enough knowledge, and they don't have the capacity to upgrade themselves. Working life is more real and has greater possibilities for training with new and modern machines.
- Industry usually has better equipment than the school. There your education is more practical. In industry you also learn how to produce.
- School can never give such an all-round training as you can get out there. There aren't real jobs for you to do. When we're at work we print big runs, and that's something you can't do at school.
- I think I learn better on the job. The work is so different from what I learned at school. When I took the foundation course at school I thought I knew all about the trade. When I began to work in the factory I came to see how little I knew.

These apprentices were in their third year and had attended apprenticeship school for eight months when I met them. As apprentices in the interview portion of my research, they voiced their discontent with learning at school. They thought that school left them far behind what actually happened in industry (see also Nilsson 1985, 19; Olsen&Seljestad 1996).

In the course of learning in most trades, there is an accumulation of one's products. For example, in the food industries bakery goods and sausages are sold; in hairdressing, customers are actually served; tailors sew for customers; and automobile mechanics repair vehicles. Another frustrating aspect of the vocational studies program was the requirement to knock down whatever constructions one had made as part of their exercises. This was especially hard to take in the building trades program. A masonry student building a brick wall, a fireplace, or a chimney in the workshop had, later, to tear it down. Carpenters building parts of a wall had to tear that down as well. As a fledgling plumber said;

> School can never give an all-rounded training like you get out there. On the job you get a better insight than at school; working out there is also more rewarding. There you're building things up. You don't knock them down (see also Olsen&Seljestad 1996, 62, 99).

## What Do I Need Theory For? I'm Going to Be a Printer

There has been an attempt to solve the contradictions between vocational training and general education by increasing the general education classroom learning component of the vocational curricula.[22] This is also one of the greatest challenges in the reform process. Vocational teachers teach and instruct in the practical subjects, technical drawing, and vocational theory, while teachers with an

22 This is another complicated field in which the signals concerning the extent and standing of general theoretical education in relation to the various trades have varied considerably in different reform periods. Wilfred Wasenden has shown in his important work how mathematics was oriented to the vocations in the 1970s (Wasenden 1995; 1997; 1999).

academic background teach the general subjects like Norwegian, social science, mathematics, physics, chemistry, and foreign languages.[23] One question to be raised here is, have there been increases in motivational problems and dropouts with this augmentation of the general education component?

Experience with the two-year foundation course, where one year of the gymnasium and one year of vocational school are combined, and where the teaching was composed of half general education and half vocational training provides an empirical basis for considering this question. The foundation course was started in Oslo in the 1970s; for example, it was initiated in the mechanical trades, electro-trades, and food industry sector in 1971. Many of the students in the two-year foundation courses had no clear idea of what they had signed up for. Many came directly from primary schooling and expected to avoid all forms of theory and 'book-learning' when they began vocational school; they were not prepared for how much general theory and classroom learning there is in vocational education. There was less competition for entering the two-year foundation courses than for the usual one-year vocational training courses. Also, for students who obtained places in the new two-year courses, this had not been their first, but rather their second or third choice.

The drop-out rate from foundation courses at Sogn Upper Secondary School in Oslo increased from 47 students in 1967 to 250–300 students per annum after 1977, or from 1 1/2 per cent to 11 per cent (Mjelde 1973/1977). (The total number of students remained the same.) The drop-out rate from some of the new, broad foundation courses after *Reform 94* seems to indicate the same tendency (Bergli 1997, 21; Kvalsund&Myklebust et al. 1998). Moreover, similar trends are documented in other research reports in Scandinavia; Boel Berner points to the same trends in vocational fields in Sweden's gymnasium school system (1989). In some classes the drop-out rate reached 70 per cent. *Forsøksrådet for skoleverket* (the Experimental Council of the

23 An increasing number of vocational teachers are now entering the field of general education as well (see Bergli 1995; 1997. See Bergli's appendices). Vocational teacher education has developed offers for vocational teachers to take up general educational teaching.

Functioning of the School) (1973) summed up the first years of this experiment as follows: 'The pupils do best in the practical subjects, while the general subjects are unpopular. Better vocational counselling is necessary. Better coordination is needed between the vocational and general subjects.' Neophyte teachers of the general subjects, fresh from the universities, were faced with these serious problems.

Counsellors in the compulsory school system are usually teachers with academic backgrounds and little knowledge of form and content in vocational education. Hans Østvold, who was secretary of the Schools Committee of 1965, said in a 1990 speech to the Society for the History of Norwegian Schooling, 'One part of the population, those who become teachers, moreover, spend their whole lives in school, and the paradox is that they are the ones given the task of preparing children and youth for life in this other society.' This is a problem arising from the social structure and is not a question of good or bad counsellors and advisors. Without trying to disparage these persons, we can point out that they have indeed had little understanding of the needs and complexities of vocational education.[24]

Boel Berner found that students who could not stand compulsory school were frequently recruited into the vocational trades. Some of these students adapted to schools with workshops, but many of them, even there, also suffered from problems of motivation (Berner 1989, 152; see also Axelsson 1989). Motivation problems in classroom learning were very noticeable in my apprenticeship investigations. The graphics apprentices had general subjects every Monday between eight in the morning and half past four in the afternoon. This consisted of two hours of Norwegian and social science, two hours of physics, two hours of mathematics, and then two hours of chemistry. During one of the Norwegian/social studies classes at eight in the morning, one of the apprentices shouted, 'To hell with this damned theory! I'm not here to listen to lies about the Third World. I'm here to learn a trade.' The teacher had assigned them group work on South Africa.

24 This is a problem that we know from the development of schooling in the past decades, whether one is located in Africa or Cuba or Norway. The Tvind School in Denmark demanded one year of practice from farm or factory work as compulsory before entering their teacher training college.

Teachers often exhibit a defensive attitude toward the problems of motivation and learning that they encounter on a daily basis. In common with the students, they have a desire to get through these classes as painlessly as possible. The teacher and the students are in constant negotiation about how much the teacher should cover, how soon until the students can take the next break. Later in the day the teacher encounters growing pressure from the apprentices who want to be released. During the last class of the day, chemistry, one of the apprentices asked; 'We've stood it for the whole day – haven't we been quiet today? Can't we go soon? We're worn out.' The chemistry teacher replied, 'I'm sorry. This is a quiet class. But why don't you learn something? You're always talking about whether it is directly useful, and if what I want to teach you is of no direct use you think it's not important.' The apprentice said, 'It's so boring. I don't understand it.'[25]

The press operators work with chemicals. The apprentices use chemicals in their everyday work in the work places and in the workshop at the vocational school. Chemistry teaching takes place in a classroom away from these work places. The apprentices fail to see any connection between what they do at the workshop and what happens during their classes in general theory. In his evaluation of *Reform* 94, Tor Bergli (1997, 25) showed that a majority of students (80 per cent) perceived no connection between workshop and classroom learning. He said that the 20 per cent who did find a connection had attributed this to 'good' teachers. Olsen and Seljestad (1996) also describe 'good teachers' as teachers who work at the integration of these different types of learning, the vocational and the general (see also Monsen 1997).

Kevin Harris (1979, 129) sums up the situation with the following characterization:

> Education mainly has to do with the negotiation of knowledge. But what I want to stress is that the function of education in liberal democratic society is to generate a destructive form of ignorance.

25 These citations are from my participant observation in the graphics class in the Apprenticeship project 1982, 84.

According to Harris, the education system stands for the development of a consumerism vis-à-vis education and an hourly wage adjustment tied directly to the acquisition of knowledge. Whatever is not spelled out in the lesson plans, and that will not be included in the examination, has no value. In vocational education one frequently hears the view 'What am I supposed to do with this?' in reference to anything not directly related to the trade (Berner 1989, 150; Faag 1997; Postman 1996). Students coming from compulsory school and into vocational schooling, as well as apprentices, are all surprised to find the same general subjects that they had to cram into their heads in school. As one of the apprentices said, 'What do I need theory for? I'm going to be a printer.'

The conclusion of one mathematics teacher is an apt summary of the need to improve co-ordination between vocational and general subjects. She said that she would need a year on the floor of a workshop in order to learn what took place there, before she could even hope to become a good mathematics and physics teacher in the vocational studies program. Then again, students in a vocational subject rebel against general subjects that 'don't have any relevance to our lives', as they put it. This is the central problem, and *Reform 94* has forced attention on it.

## Meaning, Motivation, and Learning

In order to understand what it is that creates good learning situations for students, how teaching problems arise and change for teachers, and how progress occurs, one must study more than the content of the teaching. One must also study how this is distributed and transformed in the practice of the everyday lives of the teachers and students. It is important to investigate how students and teachers view the concrete contents of the teaching, and what, from the students' and teachers' actual perspectives, are considered to be meaningful within the teaching content (Nilsson 1986). There is very little research in Scandinavia on vocational education in general, and particularly little in which the focus falls upon the everyday life of the students and the teachers.[26]

Lennart Nilsson's empirical investigations into workshop learning in Sweden during the 1970s are an exception (Nilsson 1979; 1981a&b, 1992). Nilsson shows where problem-based enquiries have been undertaken in order to come to grips both with why the students' learning difficulties arise, and into what the teaching problems are in situations where 20 to 30 per cent of the students stop attending school. He cites preliminary studies that indicate the majority of students wanted to work with assignments that had concrete applications.

As we have heard, many students considered the work they did and the learning they had undergone to be completely meaningless. What, then, would they consider to be meaningful? In what time perspective did students think and act? Were there different points of view among students in the same class? Lennart Nilsson found that what was meaningful for the learner was the character of the tasks in relation to the time perspective that the learner had in mind. There were significant variations in the time perspective of students in the same class or division. Other than by chance, the learner was unable to find meaning in his or her own task-related work.

If the work tasks are formulated in a manner that the student can carry them out within the individual's own particular concentration span, and if the student has the feeling of having succeeded at the task, then the student's breadth of knowledge and concentration in relation to the time span involved in carrying out the task is broadened and

26 There is not much prestige associated with research into vocational education. The researchers themselves have been educated far from the shop floors and the vocational schools. They have little personal acquaintance with this complex field. Ronald Sultana at the University of Malta has, however, carried out a large empirical research project on vocational education in Malta (1992; 1996). Claude Grignon (1971) carried out a large empirical research project on vocational education in France over three decades ago. These are important contributions to the field. The evaluation work concerning *Reform 94* in Norway has also been an advance. Unfortunately research into the field has stopped again in recent years. The National Research Council of Norway does not give priority to this field and the evaluation work has stopped.

extended. This makes it possible for the individual to become involved in larger and more time-consuming projects. These research results allow for new insights into what constitutes significance or 'meaningfulness' and the conditions for the progress of learning. These are important perspectives to have when it comes to a complex task, such as the preparation for learning is in all teaching situations (see also Grimestad 1993).

Today, for many students, school seems to be meaningless. There is a crisis in motivation, and discipline problems and high dropout rates are linked to this crisis (Mellin-Olsen 1989; Takala 1992; see also Båtvik, Kvalsund&Myklebust 1998, Monsen 1997). Many students have lost all desire to learn, and at the same time they have lost their confidence in their ability to learn. In everyday life we understand what motivation is. If we are asked to do something we do not like, we carry out the task very slowly. We are in a position to learn a technical process quickly if the result is meaningful, as well as rewarding and pleasurable, but we are not in a position to learn even easier tasks if we do not understand the overall purpose.

Meaning and motivation are two sides of the same coin (Enerstvedt 1987, 3; Mjelde 1993, 104–22). Regi Enerstvedt (1987) points out that the purpose in every learning process is the preparation for something else. For many, learning in school is preparation for one's participation in working life. He goes on to say that one of the main problems is the distance between school and work. Lengthening of the hours spent in pure schooling away from practical working life is one of the main problems in present-day school reforms. One of the main problems with *Reform 94* could be described as the reduction of vocational fields and workplace learning in the first year of studies, together with a lengthening to two years of the period of school attendance before one is permitted to learn a vocation (see also Bergli 1997, 52; Kvalsund&Myklebust 199; Olsen&Seljestad 1996, 64).

How are we to create an education program where the problems concerning meaning and motivation are solved? How should we present ourselves so that we do not implement a pedagogy that over-steps and avoids the contradictions between manual and intellectual labour? This presupposes a type of pedagogy with a content that tries to develop the student's scientific and general understanding of the dynamics of society. Such pedagogy ought to employ co-operation instead of competition, mutual assistance instead of individual execution, solidarity instead of self-interest, comradeship and a feeling for society instead of narrow individualism. How would a classroom look that supported some human development and forms of co-operation as mutual assistance, solidarity, and comradeship? How would a learning situation be in which everyone had an opportunity to develop his or her abilities to the optimal degree?

## Workshop Learning: How Does It Really Work?

The American psychologist Jerome Bruner wrote in 1963 that 'any subject can be taught effectively in some intellectual honest form to any child at any stage of development (Bruner 1963:33, see also Engestrøm&Hakkarainen 1981). There are many interpretations of what learning really is and how it functions among people and animals. Today the debate about this in scholarly and scientific circles is richer than every before. Learning is one of the fundamental concepts of the social sciences, and it is *the* central concept in pedagogy. Developing an understanding of how people learn is basic to organizing a pedagogical system. How, in a scientific and scholarly way, is one really to grasp the fact that vocational school students and apprentices thrive and learn things in the workshop situation and on the job, but not in the conventional academic or vocational classroom? This question has preoccupied me for the many years I have worked in the field of vocational education. In the course of trying to understand this, I have worked my way through many different theories of learning.

I have followed with interest Jerome Bruner's research in the field of education ever since he wrote an introduction to the English edition of Lev Vygotsky's 1962 book *Thought and Language*. In Bruner's book, *The Culture of Education* (1996a), he describes a discussion he had with the researcher Sylvia Scribner about 'the psychology of work' (1996, 150–51). Scribner describes how at the outset of her research project, her observation team recorded the way that the milk delivery personnel operated as they delivered their dairy products to shops and restaurants around Manhattan. She found that the particular form of problem-solving adopted by the delivery staff, how they thought, and particularly how they formulated a problem, all stemmed from the demands of the work itself. Sylvia Scribner regarded these findings as a further extension of the cognitive psychology of Lev Vygotsky.

Bruner writes that he had difficulty understanding the significance of the point she was making. He could not understand that someone might find it interesting to study how the milkman determined how many bottles of milk, cream, and yoghurt he needed for his customers. In the months that followed his meeting with Scribner, he thought a lot about their discussion. It gradually became clear to him that what may be evident in psychological terms can simultaneously conceal and preserve some of life's most important secrets. The secret here, 'if we are to generalize these findings', is that the brain (or the mind) is an extension of the means and tools one uses in working life, and at the same time is an extension of the work tasks by means of which one uses these means and tools (Bruner 1996, 151). This is analogous with the nature of learning behaviour and activity that takes place in a workshop situation.

Bruner says that a culture provides us with a rebus, in the classic sense, of cognitive activity and cognitive development. In its classic denotation, *rebus* comes from the Latin *res*, and this indicates how *things* rather than *words* can indicate what we do. Our learned forefathers understood the expression *non verbis sed rebus* (explain with things, not words), when used to convey understanding by doing something rather than by talking. Here one also finds the key to understanding why vocational students and apprentices prefer to learn by doing. Another facet of learning by doing is the fact that something is done together with either a teacher or master, and with other fellow learners.

In more recent theories of learning, major weight has been placed upon the basic nature of mutual or reciprocal effects in the learning process. Learning has come to be seen not as something that occurs in a student's head while she/he is listening to a teacher or reading a book, but rather as something that is fundamentally mutual. Learning is 'the internalization of schemata', schemata which integrate cognition with perception and activity. Schemata are made meaningful by means of one doing something together with an 'expert' in such a manner that the learner gradually masters ever more difficult parts of the task at hand. Gradually she/he becomes more capable of carrying out more complex tasks until she/he no longer requires the assistance of the expert. Learning based on common activity leads to the gradual mastery of more difficult tasks by the novice (Goody 1989, 253; Enkenberg 1994).[27] We can refer to this process as a master-apprenticeship model. There is a master-apprenticeship model in workshop learning as shown in Figure 5 below.

The advantage in vocational education has been a pedagogy based on learning from practice to theory, as well as the proximity between learning and working life. What is special about vocational education is that the work of the mind is formed by the work of the hand, and that in the learning process one moves from action to thought. Here the student learns through the fundamental work processes, through manual practice. The dynamic between theory and practice moves from the practical to the theoretical and back again such that hand and mind are in a dialectical relationship. Understanding comes through activity, reciprocity, and personal experience, and theory is learned in close relationship with practical ability. The vocational school is based on this model. Students provide a skilled service or make something real – the workshop is the main arena for learning. They bake bread, make sausages, build houses, cut and style hair, repair television sets. Learning takes place amid the roar of machinery or the blast of hot ovens.

27 The basis upon which this flowering of understanding has arisen is the working out of Lev Vygotsky's important works on learning in the Soviet Union in the 1920s. Work in this tradition has been a great source of inspiration to me (Mjelde 1993, 33–39).

| WORKSHOP | WORKSHOP/ CLASSROOM | LECTURE HALL/ CLASSROOM |
|---|---|---|

| PRACTICE: | VOCATIONAL THEORY: | GENERAL THEORY: |
|---|---|---|
| Kitchen | Technical drawing | Norwegian |
| Mechanical Workshop | Knowledge of materials | Mathematics |
| Building site | Braking theory | Natural sciences |
| Hospital ward | Social & Caring fields | English |
| | Human biology | |
| | etc. | |

Figure 5: Arenas of Learning in Vocational Education

It is important to stress that the students can work together and consult one another while the teacher goes around the room advising and instructing each group of practitioners at their various levels of the work process. Co-operation with the teacher and with other students is fundamental to the learning process (see also Dyrdal 1995). It is significant that vocational education has its own particular values. When a teacher and fifteen students spend several hours together in a workshop, whether it be a kitchen or a garage, the relationship between teacher and student, and between student and student is different from what we normally find with class time in a lecture hall (see also Faag 1997).[28]

28 As production processes have developed, one of the problems has been a reduction of workshop learning and also a reduction of the vocational teachers' course load. Arising from a demand that all teachers have the same course load, workshop teaching has been significantly weakened. On the other hand, academic teachers have a difficult teaching situation. They can have over one hundred students a week (see also Blichfeldt 1992).

In the workshop, the functioning of body and mind are not separated, with the bodies of the learners immobilized in a sitting position and arranged in rows in front of the teacher. In workshop learning these bodies and minds work together. The learners move around with the rhythms of the work. Traditional school values, which declare among other things that working together signals a form of cheating, are absent from the value system in vocational education. In the work situation, weight is placed on mutual dependence. Before the enactment of legislation on upper secondary schooling in 1974, marks were not awarded in the industrial subjects; only pass or fail were used in grading the practical examinations. Nonetheless, we see that the contradictions between mental and manual labour persist in vocational education with its division into three components: workshop learning, vocational theory, and general theory (Nilsson 1981, 37).

General theory, Norwegian, mathematics, physics, and social science are taught in the academic classroom. Students sit in rows facing the teacher, who is located at the front behind a desk. Learning activity is expected to be individualized and internalized, in the mind. There is little relationship between what is taught and learned in the academic classroom and what is taught in the workshop and in vocational theory. Clearly, these are two quite different ways of organizing learning.[29] In the workshop model, and the relationship between workshop learning and vocational theory, where the gulf between mental and manual activities is being crossed, we can perhaps see the beginning of the education of the future (Mjelde 1996a).[30] Workshop learning is the foundation for learning by means of activity and cooperation. Vocational theory, on the other hand,

29 It is obvious that in general much of the academic teaching has developed toward the workshop model. Pupils/students sit in a horseshoe arrangement; teachers instruct less from the front of the classroom, and use more time to go around the room guiding the learners (see Lindblad 1997).

30 I am of course speaking here about the form and not the content. The content is another and complex question. I did a curriculum criticism of the contents in the social science textbook in 1972 and ended up writing and alternative textbook (Mjelde 1975) See also Jerome S. Bruner (1963 115-126) 'After John Dewey,What?'

includes language, mathematics, physics, and chemistry – in short, general theory (Wasenden 1997, 1999).

Vocational theory (see Figure 1, page 35), taught in both the workshop and the classroom, has varied over time in accordance with the development of and changes in the content of the various vocations.[31] Vocational theory is closely connected to the content and development of the various trades. The goal in vocational theory is to communicate knowledge about tools, materials and processes within each vocation. Industrial or mechanical drawing, for example, is a substantial part of much of vocational theory in the fields of the crafts and industry. The general subjects lack, in terms of content, direct connection with the part of vocational education that deals with the technical aspects of the work, and they also lack connection to vocational theory. As an electrician in an apprenticeship programme (1982–84) that I monitored wrote, 'School can't give you realistic teaching, neither for the trades nor for the general subjects.' In vocational education, there is a destructive or even ruinous relationship between the manual labour trades portion and the general education portion, between the workshop and the classroom lectures, between the individual and the group. In short, the destructive gap between the hand and the mind is plain to see. But by honestly analysing these contradictions arising between the different learning traditions, we can find ways of posing new questions about how to correct and improve both the teaching and the learning.

One of the main challenges created by *Reform 94* is, how can we possibly link the general subjects with workshop learning and vocational theory? Today, students learn the theorems of Pythagoras as geometry, as general theory, rather than, for example, in the context of how a carpenter uses Pythagoras in building a house. When carpenters calculate an angle, they are applying Pythagorean theorems. Why can they not learn Pythagoras as they learn to calculate or measure an angle with the tools of their intended trade? (see also

31 This is a composite field in the development of the vocations, with great variations within the crafts and industry, and between the crafts and industry/caring professions and the home economics/aesthetic fields. The basis for my comments here are primarily the fields of crafts and industry.

Wasenden 1995, 1999). Printers use chemicals every day. Why could a teacher of the natural sciences not work together in the same place with the workshop teacher? Why could she/he not teach about the chemicals that one uses in the graphics field on an everyday basis? Student cooks learn the principles and formulas of the functioning of flame, steam, and biochemistry when they are in the academic classroom, while they actually experience the application of this knowledge, albeit unconsciously, in practice in the kitchen. Ratios of temperature, and selection and quantities of ingredients learned in the kitchen seem distant from the principles of biochemistry learned in the classroom. Why could the natural science teacher not work together with the teacher of cooking to teach the principles and formulas in the kitchen? We have seen promising examples of such trends. Mikkel Bongo (1998) followed a cohort of adults at an adult education centre over the course of one year. Here the relationships were set out for vocational pedagogical learning by means of extensive cooperation between the vocational and the academic teachers. The evaluation reports reveal great ingenuity and desire in the effort to integrate vocational and academic subjects (Bergli 1997, 17; Olsen&Seljestad 1996, 64–65; Olsen 2000; Wasenden 2001).

This is not a new issue in the field of education. It has been at the core in the discussion for over a century. In the next chapter I discuss these questions in relation to the work of two great pedagogical thinkers, Lev Vygotsky and John Dewey.

CHAPTER 4

# Learning and Meaning in Vocational Education: Lev Vygotsky and John Dewey on Vocational Pedagogy

One of the main findings of my research in the vocational sector is that the students and apprentices in the vocational trades prospered and learned when they were active in the workplace, but they found no meaning or relevance to the classroom hours of general academic education. So, they showed up for the workshop classes but not for the academic classes. Why have vocational students' and apprentices' experiences of learning and meaning in the workshop setting and working life contrasted so sharply with those of the school with its classrooms?

## The Organization of Teaching in Vocational Education

In the course of its history, vocational education in the crafts and industries branch has employed many different methods for organizing workshop, vocational theoretical, and general teaching. As explained above, vocational schooling for crafts and industry took working life as its model until the *Upper Secondary Schooling Act* came into effect in 1976. Forty-two hours a week was common in the training for many trades. Between 1945 and 1976, the model saw two-thirds of the teaching time devoted to workshop instruction and one-third to general education in the classroom. There were various ways of arranging this.

At the Elvebakken Vocational School in Oslo in the early 1970s, the teaching was organized with one week in the workshop and the next week in the academic classroom. In this way, it was possible to have two groups alternating the use of the workshops. The boys showed up for the weeks in the workshop but not for those in the academic classroom where the teachers of the academic subjects often sat alone at their desks (Bjerketvedt, Helltorp&Mjelde 1971). The teachers also frequently faced a difficult working situation in terms of the vocational curriculum. They might teach up to one hundred students each week – students for very different trades – and many of these were very lightly motivated to learn theory. What was the reason for the hostility the students had developed toward what they called 'theory'? Two quotations from my apprenticeship study 1982–1984 show this division very plainly: A graphics student said, 'You learn more by working (in practice) than by sitting in a school desk with all that baloney about theory.' A mechanic's apprentice said, 'It was terrific to get away from sitting at that school desk where you're just supposed to accept stuff. Finally we could produce something ourselves. Working and earning money for three years suits me much better. And also, I was sick and tired of school' (Mjelde 1993, 103).

'Tired of school' and 'sick of school' were expressions which came up again and again among the 1,617 apprentices in the study. Eighty-nine per cent preferred being apprentices to sitting at a school desk. As one of them put it, 'Going to school in today's society really takes it out of you.' This apprentice, in Bergen, had experienced his everyday school life as a nightmare. Research into the primary schools of the 1970s revealed that 20 per cent of the students were bullied or bullied other students. This is not a new phenomenon in the development of schooling, but it becomes ever more serious as the length of obligatory schooling increases.

There have been many attempts to give primary school an orientation more in accord with the pedagogy of work, from the days of Anna Sethne in the Sagene district of Oslo in the 1930s to the present. Conflict arises in the school debate every day about these matters. However, primary schooling today still seems to be marked by the scholastic Latin school traditions with atomized teaching. Such teaching is characterized by a lack of connection between the various subjects, between the students, and by classes that continue to be forty-five minutes long, such that the school day is punctuated only by the ringing of the bell. The school is, of course, a sorting mechanism where achievements and marks lay the basis for broader vocational choices and places in working life. It is one of the sorting gates that stream the student toward either the vocational trades or the academic professions after the conclusion of the compulsory primary schooling.

However, this is not the main point I wish to make here. I present it only as background in order to pose questions about meaning and meaninglessness in the pedagogy that is pursued, whether it be in primary school, in vocational training, or in higher education. Yet, it is the basis for posing questions both about primary school and vocational training for the crafts and industry branches of the economy, particularly when as many as 89 per cent of the apprentices in my apprenticeship study of 1982–84 (Mjelde 1993) found the learning arenas in school to be meaningless.

Is the fact that the existing learning situations in the schools are viewed by many of the students as irrelevant and meaningless one of the main problems for the development of schooling over the past thirty years? Has the division between learning at the workplace and learning in the classroom, as it has developed over the past thirty years, contributed to a refusal to learn among those participating in vocational courses of study? Has the increase in the proportion of general classroom education, as in the conventional basic school system with everybody seated in rows, has this led to an increase in the problems faced by vocational education? Briefly:

- Is it the social conditions of the school which contribute to the students being unable to learn?
- How should these social relations be corrected such that all have optimal learning conditions in any particular learning situation?

Lennart Nilsson is one of the few researchers in Scandinavia who has worked with the problems of learning and teaching in relation to vocational education.[32] He points out that there has been little interest

32 Tove Lien (1984; 1995) has carried out empirical investigations concerning these questions in the context of adult education. In relation to the labour

in the empirical study of how students in the vocational trades experience their learning conditions and possibilities. He maintains that this sort of study is a prerequisite for the future. Furthermore, one has to take these student experiences seriously by approaching teaching in such a way that it conveys what, from the perspective of the students, gives meaning to the work. To experience education as something meaningful is a starting point for the development of competence and adjustment to the work situation (Nilsson 1981).

The apprentices in my apprenticeship study of 1982–84 (Mjelde 1993) had experienced their learning as meaningless and irrelevant, both in the compulsory school years and in the general academic teaching for the foundation course in their chosen vocational field. Students in the first empirical study I conducted in the vocational schools in Oslo in the 1970s felt that they had 'come home' when they experienced workshop learning in their vocational training (see p. 29 above). Klaus Nielsen and Steinar Kvale point to the metaphorical similarity between the psychological and social development of the child, on one hand, and the content of the apprenticeship legislation, on the other: 'Through their participation in everyday life, both the child and the apprentice get to observe and participate in the activities of the 'master' – either the mother or father, or the instructor in the firm that is the workplace' (1999, 133). In earlier work, I have placed more emphasis upon the cultural aspects of this problem. Students come to a culture they know from home, a culture of work with specific norms and values. They know the language and the 'rules of the game', and they have gained this understanding in the course of their daily lives (Mjelde 1987; 1993).

Accordingly, one way of comprehending these dilemmas lies in understanding that there are two quite different arenas of learning, the workshop and the general education classroom, and this division is very plainly observed in the development of the various vocational courses of study. The workshops are imitations of actual workplaces, and here the teacher functions as a working foreman/master of the

---

market, and whether carried out at school or at adult education centres, vocational education in the crafts and industry trades are two sides of the same coin.

trade (Mjelde, 1987). The student's learning time is organized similar to the working day rather than to the time division in the classroom. General education subjects are taught in conventional classrooms. The day is divided into forty-five-minute periods and the students often have six different subjects in one day. In the workshop situation they learn in a holistic manner that is based on physical activity and interaction. General education is built up in a 'traditional presentation' with strong divisions between academic subjects. The teacher works from the logical configuration and structure of the individual subject, and this, together with the goals of the lesson plans forms the starting point for atomistic teaching.

Vocational school students and apprentices find no relationship in the content of the three parts of the teaching they receive in their vocational field – workshop learning, vocational theory, and general education. Mikkel Bongo has pointed out that students in the vocational trades are unable to find any relationship between one chapter and the next in the same textbook in their academic subjects, such as, for example, the chapters on energy in their physics text (2001b).[33]

Today, students enter training for the vocations after ten years of compulsory schooling. Many of them have been in a school situation where they have fallen behind. Many have not learned to read and write properly, or cannot perform even the most rudimentary arithmetic calculations. They have fallen out of the education spiral early on. This falling behind is a cumulative process. If the student does not learn the basic principles upon which a school subject rests, and begins to fall behind, the distance becomes greater and greater between what the student knows and necessary preparation for higher, more complex levels of knowledge toward which the student and her/his classmates are expected to be advancing. Once they have fallen behind, they lose confidence in their ability to learn. Knud Illeris maintains that 'in adult education in Denmark one very often

33 Mikkel Bongo kindly read a draft of this manuscript and has given me constructive criticism based upon his experience as principal of a large secondary school which has both academic and vocational courses of study, and is based upon his own research (he wrote a graduate thesis in vocational pedagogy in 1998).

encounters participants who have such a negative attitude toward the education that they experienced during their school years, and who must be won over before one can speak at all about any meaningful educational progress' (1999, 81–82). The same situation occurs in adult education in Norway (Lien 1984, 1991, 1995, Bongo 1998).[34]

But back to our starting point: Why do vocational students thrive and learn in the workshops that are integral to vocational courses of study? What in particular is it about this learning situation that makes it different from the classroom tradition of education? What is it that creates an atmosphere for learning and cooperation? How can this be understood scientifically from what we now know about learning? Two men of science and scholarship who have been involved in laying the foundations for such understanding are Lev Vygotsky and John Dewey.[35]

## Lev Vygotsky and Vocational Pedagogy

Both human beings and animals learn, but what in particular is the trajectory of development for human learning, a learning that begins at birth and continues until death? How have human languages, thoughts, and consciousness come into being? What is the characteristic difference between learning among people and learning among the apes?

34 Knud Illeris (1999, 65-68) seems to have a somewhat romantic view of the construction of this opposition, both in relation to the good learning situation and to what he calls 'popular [folk] opposition'. He finds constructive features to this opposition from biological and psychological perspectives. I am sceptical about this interpretation. I believe that the school's oppression of human potential for learning creates unhealthy conditions for learning, and often for compassionate fellow human beings.

35 Jean Piaget is of course important when it comes to our understanding of learning processes. However, I have not gone into his contribution here because he does not directly address the field of vocational didactics.

We find a point of entry to understanding this problematic in the works of Lev Vygotsky.[36] He provided a historical analysis of the development of the higher mental functions of the human being. A major feature of Vygotsky's thinking is that a human being learns in a certain definite direction; namely, from the social to the individual. People develop their mental and psychic activity through speech. Thinking and language cannot profitably be studied in isolation but ought to be viewed from a social and developmental perspective. The psychological development of the individual is dependent upon the historical epoch in which this development occurs. A. R. Luria (1976) and A. N. Leontiev (1978) have further illuminated this phenomenon by showing the variation in the development of consciousness in relation to geographical conditions and social background (Daly&Mjelde 2000; Mjelde 1987; 1993). This point of view is of fundamental significance for all pedagogy. It indicates that the child is not to be viewed first and foremost as a biological being to be socialized through norms and values so as to develop his or her cognition. Rather, the child is a social being who develops her/himself through human interaction and language, through the internalization of the norms and the acquisition of whatever knowledge is particular to when in history and where on earth that child is living.[37]

36 Lev Vygotsky has been called the Mozart of psychology (Toulmin 1978). He was long forgotten but has had a great influence on research into learning during the past thirty-year period. His book *Thought and Language* came out in English in 1962 and *Mind and Society* came out in 1978. His thinking had also been 'forgotten' for a long period of time in the Soviet Union. Thought and Language [Tenkning og tale] came out in Norwegian in 2001. Jerome Bruner's works on teaching and learning have been influenced by the thinking of Lev Vygotsky from as far back as the early 1960s (Bruner 1996b). The works of Jean Lave and Etienne Wenger on master-apprentice traditions seem to have their origin in Vygotsky's scientific thinking.

37 In a lecture presented in Kristiansand in 1992, Per Strømholm stressed the historically varying nature of our feelings and thoughts. He took an interesting polemical position against the assertion by Norway's Nobel prize-winning writer, Sigrid Undset, that our human feelings are eternal and unchanging. He characterized her novel *Kristin Lavransdatter*, set in the Middle Ages, as a modern woman's novel in which she had transferred twentieth-century thinking and modes of being to people of the fourteenth century.

Consequently, language and communication are fundamental both to human mental activity and to the development of each human generation in each society. The human being has developed language, thought, and consciousness through work (activity) and cooperation. Vygotsky uses the concepts of *word* and *meaning* as basic tools for investigating the development of language and thought processes. A person does not learn a word's significance without the word being associated with its meaning (its socially created connotations [contextual meanings] and denotations [generalized or abstract meaning]). Individual experience can only be communicated beyond the experience of the individual when it is organized into categories that are confirmed and verified by other participants in society through established conventions and customs. Meaning is composed of units of these implicitly common categories. The generalizations or denotations that are implicit in the categories simplify experience.

Without simplifications and symbols to organize them, the higher forms of human interaction and cooperation would not be possible. Society needs systems of mediation for determining and categorizing what is rational and intentional in the actions and thoughts of its members. This system of mediation is language, where the basic units are words and meanings. Thus, words and meanings are tools developed through verbal and written interactions between members of society. In the course of striving to understand one another, members of society create new internal monologues in which their own experiences are measured against and contrasted with the conventions and generalizations of the society and culture (see Voloshinov 1973; Smith 1999, 96–130).

*Meaning* and *real life understanding* are core concepts for philosophers of language such as V. N. Voloshinov and L. Wittgenstein. These philosophers of language argue that in normal everyday life meaning is seldom denotative; it is not abstract or general; nor is it separated from a living social context. In a word, everyday meaning is always special and concrete (Mjelde 1993, 35).

These considerations can be directly related to the experiences that vocational students and apprentices have acquired from the learning arenas of present-day society, and their grasp of learning in the school tradition versus learning in the tradition of working life. In the school tradition, learning is separated from the real, local, concrete, contextualized understanding of life and of the concrete nature of everyday existence. This is quite different from the traditions of vocational training. On the other hand, one clearly sees how the development of vocational education at school, divided between the vocational trades on one side, and the general subjects on the other, is a development that has led to the impoverishment of education in the vocational trades. The hallmark of workshop learning in the field of vocational pedagogy is the relationship between concrete activities. Actions, words, and meanings are integrated and stand together in the learning process. The learner has a distinct experience of meaningfulness as she/he learns.[38]

Another aspect of vocational pedagogy is the learning that occurs in the course of interacting and co-operating with others. Vygotsky maintained that the thinking processes of any individual must be understood as a form of internal speech that has been transferred and internalized from its starting point in social interaction. His point of departure is that the learner moves dialectically between spontaneous self-reflective learning and a more scientific and logically oriented form of learning. Concepts that children learn spontaneously on their own, by participating in spoken interactions with other human beings, are what he refers to as 'everyday concepts'. On the other hand, those ideas and concepts that the child acquires through an explicit and systematic assimilation of the material to be learned, into what she/he already knows, are called 'intellectual' or 'scientific concepts', and are frequently defined theoretically with the help of other words. For example, an everyday term like 'dog' can be put through a hierarchy of scientific concepts such as animal, vertebrate, mammal, and canine (Vygotsky 2001a, 13). The learner's appropriation of a word's general and comparative meaning is extremely dependent upon being put into a special context. If the learner has not experienced a certain life

38 I am not saying that the relationship between meaning, meaninglessness, and learning is solved in vocational education, far from it. The deep split between workshop learning, vocational theory, and general classroom teaching is just as destructive of vocational education now as it has been earlier in history. What I am stressing is that we now understand these contradictions to a greater degree than ever before (Mjelde 1997a; Sultana 1997).

situation, the learner's comprehensions of the words that generalize experience remain incomplete until everyday life introduces experiences that give a greater depth of understanding to that particular generalizing word. This process takes place in the most immediate zone of development, in the necessary interplay between the learner's inductive experience (which gives rise to word sense) and the deductive, generalizing, teacher-directed instruction (which helps expand understanding of generalized word meanings). If one is lacking in rich experience with the multi-facetted nature of words and their significance, one does not learn to evaluate a word's full meaning in one's society, culture, and historical moment (Daly&Mjelde 2000).

Lev Vygotsky criticized traditional teaching from the point of view of his understanding of the great importance of interaction and cooperation in the processes of learning. He argued that the learner's ongoing performance in interaction with the teacher and fellow students was a far more precise index of learning than intelligence tests based upon a goal composed of pre-digested knowledge.[39] It is therefore his concept of 'the zone of proximal development' which directly addresses the workshop learning and master-teacher tradition, such as that we can observe in vocational training within the crafts and industry sector. Vygotsky's own definition of 'the zone of proximal development' is as follows: 'It is the distance between the actual developmental level as determined by independent problem solving and the level of potential development as determined through problem solving under adult guidance or in collaboration with more capable peers' (1978, 86).

American researchers have developed the notion of 'scaffolding' to describe this process. The concept is taken from the scaffold on a building site. The scaffolding is the support that the child or the adult gets in the process of solving a task with which she/he can potentially cope. In the same sense that a scaffold at a building site is a temporary structure, a scaffolding of assistance for the learning student is equally provisional. It is there to help the student carry out the assigned task,

39 In earlier works, I have criticized the definition of intelligence as a tautology: 'Intelligence is what one measures with intelligence tests' (Kokkersvold& Mjelde 1982).

and then to be taken away. The scaffolding can also be interpreted from the perspective of the teacher also being active within the learning process together with the students; that is, the teacher here sets definite goals for the students' learning activity. Stig Mellin-Olsen (1989; see also Mellin-Olsen&Solvang 1978) has developed this concept in relation to, among other things, mathematical instruction. He uses the concept of scaffold building for the process that a teacher sets into motion when he or she gives guidance. The goal is to get the learning process underway so as to hand over the accomplishment to the learner and thereby tear down the scaffolding.

Moll (1990, 3–15) argues that it is the following aspects of Vygotsky's theory that have significance for understanding the zone of proximal development: holistic teaching and mediated (mediating and bringing about) learning and change. By 'mediated learning' he means that words and language are the tools that act as intermediaries and bring about internal human activity. Vygotsky criticized traditional teaching for having an atomistic view of learning. Among other things, he felt that both the splitting up of the school subjects and the parcelling out of teaching content into individual subjects contributed to the elimination of the meaningfulness of the individual subjects. Knowledge, he argued, cannot be taken out of its natural context and passed on in isolation; it can only yield meaning and create motivation if it is taken up as a part of a whole. Another of his major principles is that learning occurs through the internalization of processes that, in the first place, the individual carries out together with others in her/his surroundings or habitat. As an alternative to traditional mediatory pedagogy, Vygotsky proposed a form of teaching that involved the development of higher psychological processes through an active co-operation between the teacher and the student collective, and which stimulates each individual to attain a new level of personal development.

Vygotsky was an educational optimist and believed that reflexive consciousness came to the learner through scientific concepts. With this point of view in mind, Bruner maintained, in his book *The Process of Education*, 'Any subject can be taught effectively in some intellectually honest form to any child at any stage of development ... Correct and illuminating explanations are no more difficult and often easier to understand than ones that are partly correct and therefore too complicated or too restricted' (1963, 23 see also Mjelde 1986; Illeris 1999).

## John Dewey and Vocational Pedagogy

There are similarities but also great differences in the ways that Lev Vygotsky and John Dewey approached these questions. When it comes to the view of relations between activity and the development of learning they have common ideas, especially with regard to the roles played by everyday activities and social relations in the education process. These perspectives directly affect the questions that are at the core of vocational pedagogy.[40]

The school system has a teaching plan that implies advancing a scientific mode of thinking. But to judge from the experiences of vocational students and apprentices, one can question whether the scientific and analytical mode of thought is advanced to even the most modest degree in the schools of today. Has the division in learning between practical and theoretical subjects made the development of scientific and analytical thinking impossible? John Dewey answered this in the affirmative in his critique of the school system a full hundred years ago. Dewey's development of holistic teaching which he argued must have its point of departure in the workshops, only served to confirm the unscientific nature of thinking fostered by the existing school system, both at the end of the 1800s and again now, a century later. In his book *School and Society* (1900), he maintained that there is a great difference of motivation, spirit, and atmosphere in

40 With regard to this, I do not place great weight on the differences, although I am not saying they are irrelevant to these important questions today. Dewey was in the Soviet Union in 1928, project-based teaching was one of his 'trademarks' and it seems to have been rejected by the Soviets at the end of the 1920s (see Glassmann 2001).

those schools where occupations are made the distinct centre of the school's life.

Learning by doing is a well-known concept that came out of Dewey's laboratory school research in Chicago. Another of Dewey's relevant perspectives is important in this context: 'There is a form of fruitless theory that stands opposed to practice. But real scientific theory is located within practice and functions as the impetus for expansion and provides direction toward new possibilities' (see Dewey and Dewey 1915, Dewey 1916).

Today's vocational students and apprentices see little or no relation between what they learn in the workshop/workplace and in the classroom; they rebel against theory and comparative concepts that seem to have nothing to do with their own reality. Vocational theory that should be linked directly to the activities of the workshop is frequently relegated to the classroom instead of to the learner's vocational practice. How can things be corrected so that good learning processes are established where learning and developing happen in tandem and in relation to one another?

Dewey promoted workshop learning and cooperation in his works. He broke with all the usual formalism in the organization of teaching. He broke with the system of school classes, school lessons, and school subjects. He stressed interdisciplinary approaches, especially through experimentation. By means of the experiments, the students would deny or confirm the hypotheses they had put forward. They acquired knowledge about the circumstances to which the experiment was related. To a considerable degree, theory became linked to practice. Dewey formulated it as follows:

> Take the textile industry as an example of such a hypothesis. I am now talking about a school that we hope to have in the future. It consists of a work room where one engages in real things, one sews spins and weaves. Children come directly in contact with work, with different types of silk, cotton, linen and wool. One gains knowledge while one works with the material, its origins, measurements and use, and the different types of machines that are used to refine the raw materials (Dewey 1916).

Hilde Jangård has pointed out that what is needed in the school system is not to offer the youth less theory, but to present theory linked to practice. She gave the interesting example of a vocational teacher who assigned, as an examination project for his students in an electrical trades class, the task of first making a technical drawing of integrated circuits and second of carrying out the task in practice. Most of the students were unable to do the assignment. Previously the teacher had given the students the same task, the difference being that he had on that occasions asked them first to carry out the practical task, and then make the drawing of what they had done. Eleven out of twelve students managed to do this in a satisfactory manner, but they were unable to work in the opposite direction, from the abstract realm to the practical. This is a typical example of what she called 'the popular learning tradition',[41] where practice and theory are carried out in an integrative and inductive manner (1978: p.104).

Jangård's observation of the teaching of the electrical trades in the 1970s, and Vygotsky's and Dewey's contributions toward the understanding of learning and teaching, give us new insights into the contradictions involved in learning in school, as experienced by vocational students and apprentices. If we look at these ideas in relation to the traditions of workshop learning it is easy to see that in this type of learning things happen through activity, interaction, and cooperation. The pedagogy that has its point of departure the work of the hand in relation to workshop learning gives us a basis for speaking about a unique process for acquiring new knowledge and gaining the direct experience useful for later comparative knowledge acquisition.

Students learn by cooperating with teachers and other students. They learn through work activities. Hand and mind stand in a dialectical relationship to one another in the learning process itself. One learns not only with the head, because the whole body is in activity. The teacher demonstrates and teaches, and goes from student to student instructing them in the use of materials and machinery. Students work together on their technical tasks. Learning occurs in processes where the learner carries out actions together with a more

41 It is interesting to see that this concept also appears in Bruner's book, *The Culture of Education*, 1996a, where Chapter 2 is called 'Folk Pedagogy'.

competent person. The teacher and the student undergo a co-operative activity regarding any given task. The teacher demonstrates and the student tries to replicate what she/he has been shown. Learning occurs by the power of example, where the teacher embodies the competency of the trade that the learner is trying to make her or his own. The students' co-operation on working tasks also constitutes a real learning resource – they learn from one another.

Workshop evaluation is process-oriented and occurs in the form of an immediate feedback of concrete results. Within what is known as the master-teaching tradition, Nielsen and Kvale (1999, 208–209) distinguish between evaluations based on consequence and those based upon utility. The apprentice learns directly from the consequences of her/his learning activities. The apprentice in an industrial firm gets direct feedback about whether or not he has completed an assignment correctly. The components that the apprentices produce have to be of professionally high standard if they are to advance further in the production process.

A mistake in an aircraft mechanic apprentice's work can have grave consequences – the aircraft can plummet from the sky and crash. The work of auto mechanics has similar dimensions. When an apprentice's work has such immediate consequences for the community of practice, what the person concerned do is also filled with gravity and significance. Such work requires precision, honesty, and dependability. Ethics is not something one sits down to learn in a classroom. Ethics is something one learns through practice, and the honing of skills and the work ethic are built right into the trade or vocation (Mjelde 2000; Tempte 1982).

In many trades one finds an ongoing and inbuilt utility evaluation of the products and services. The whole activity group stands responsible when the client or customer evaluates the products. The cooking students prepare the meal under the guidance of the master, and the waiters co-operate with the cooks to get the food to the guests. The quality of the food, its appearance, taste, and expedition are then subject to the evaluation of the guests. If the vocational student in the bakery has made a mistake in the preparation of the bread dough, the sale of bread will fall off. If a sewing student in the textile line makes a wrong cut in the fabric, the garment has to be discarded. If quality decreases, customers are lost. In such situations the workers and learners are responsible for one another's learning and performance. Being responsible for your own learning is not sufficient; the results of the learning of the group also have to be considered. The experience of the whole activity/praxis group depends upon the participants being responsible for the results of their own learning and performance as well as that of the others.

## Paradoxes and Dilemmas

The 'master teacher', 'situated learning', 'social learning' and 'learning by doing' are now important concepts in the academic debate about learning. To cite the Norwegian-Danish professor Steinar Kvale (1993), the master teacher has been rehabilitated. Nielsen and Kvale's book *Mesterlære: Læring som sosial praksis* (The Master Teacher: Learning as Social Practice, 1999) focuses upon the traditional form of master-teacher pedagogy and its relevance to the modern pedagogical problematic. The work of social anthropologists Jean Lave and Etienne Wenger has had a great influence on the direction that thought has taken on this theme in Denmark. Another anthology entitled '*Apprenticeship: From Theory to Method and Back Again'* (Coy et al. 1989) is the result of another group of social anthropologists taking up the theme of learning (by doing and through social relations) as the contributors observed in many different learning situations around the globe. All of these works take Lev Vygotsky's work as the point of departure.

A paradigm shift has been talked about in the field of teacher education and in the universities in relation to teaching and learning (Gulbrandsen, 1994; Waage, 1995). 'Problem-based learning' 'project-oriented teaching', and 'activity reflection' are concepts in this debate. Concepts such as 'experiential learning', 'self-responsibility in learning', and 'project-oriented teaching' are also central concepts in the reforms of secondary schooling. One of the major problems with a number of these concepts is that they are not always directly applicable in a vocational context, or they simply recommend the obvious. 'Project-oriented teaching' has always been organically integral to the vocational tradition. 'Responsibility for everybody's learning' is a part of vocational pedagogy and comes into conflict with concepts such as 'responsibility for one's own learning'. Everyone is naturally responsible for her or his own learning. But what does this slogan mean for students and teachers in their everyday life? Askerøi and Høie (1999, 128–30) discusses the dilemmas arising from the phrase 'responsibility for one's own learning' in terms of the demands that are placed on the students with regard to forms of examinations and exam results. What is it that leads and directs the acquisition of knowledge and learning? 'Knowledge and know-how', 'attitudes', and 'skills and proficiency' are other slogans for how the school system should develop the potentials of its students. The concept of ethics has also come forward and joined the everyday life of the school. Students ought to learn about ethics. But, simply put, if one is not responsible and ethical, one will be a danger and a menace as an auto mechanic or an air mechanic, and probably will be unemployable. This responsibility quite naturally enters into the daily reality of a workshop, yet many would have severe difficulty sitting in a classroom and studying about the ethics of work (Mjelde 2000).

The following is one dilemma which has to do with vocational branches of study and which arises from *Reform 94*: It appears that as a result of the reforms, workshop learning has been weakened, while classroom learning has increased and expanded. This is counter to everything that experience teaches us about the way schooling has developed in recent decades, and that research into education and learning has indicated. Workshop practice has been reduced to eleven hours a week in the foundation courses and the general education portion has increased proportionally. Students must now go to school for two years before they are eligible to apply for an apprenticeship. Britt Ulstrup-Engelsen points out that for many students who formerly 'jumped out of the system' after the comprehensive/junior high school years and found them self some vocational training, it was precisely the lack of similarity with their earlier school experience that they found so liberating (1999). Have the classroom traditions of the compulsory school increased with *Reform 94*? Have the problems of learning and motivation increased in vocational education at school with the increase in the amount of required general education?

The evaluation reports on *Reform 94* discuss several trends that it has encouraged: the tendency that the courses of study in the vocational trades are in the process of shifting from workplace learning and are being marked more and more by academic schooling, the general extension of classroom teaching by an extra two years *before* apprenticeships and workshop instruction is allowed, the greater proportion of expected general classroom learning, and the use of models that have little or no relevance (Bergli 1997, Olsen 1996, Olsen et al. 1998). This is happening side by side with the use of terms and slogans derived from the learning traditions of vocational pedagogy, and these terms are being enshrined in teaching plans and curriculum outlines. The concept of vocational didactics is now part of the Department of Education's teaching syllabus for upper secondary education. Teaching plans indicate that there is to be a proportional division between practice and theory of 60 per cent practice and 40 per cent theory in the first year of vocational programs of study. How this is being carried out in practice has been shown to be extremely complicated (Leithe 1995, Riiber 1997).

Bongo has raised the paradox that many vocational teachers believe that vocational theory can only be learned in a classroom (2001b). He gave the example of the way a vocational teacher demonstrated in a classroom beside the workshop how one warms up and bends a pipe. The teacher had obviously thought that the course of studies required that this be done 'theoretically', which has not been the case either before or since *Reform 94*. Bongo went on to say that a great number working in the upper secondary school do not grasp the possibilities given by the new syllabus plans.

The *Reform 94* evaluation reports also reveal the structural features of the organization of teaching which hinder the development of both teaching and learning (Blichfeldt et al. 1999). There is much to hinder the success of the learning process: lesson plans, differences in teaching duties for teachers in the general and vocational education sectors, different reading tasks for teachers conducting workshop instruction, and vocational theory teaching. The structure of general education is problematic for the vocational lines in the larger combined schools. Five lessons in each subject are laid out parallel to one another so that all the academic students can have the opportunity to choose vocational subjects. The result is that, in a subject requiring lessons of two or three hours (and these are overwhelmingly vocational subjects), that particular course of studies suffers. Lessons in these subjects are forced to end when academic lessons do. As well, these lessons are frequently scheduled for inconvenient times during the school day. Bongo furthermore has pointed out that there is little status for university-educated teachers to teach in the vocational lines where their specialty subject is reduced to an 'application' or a 'tool', and where, in addition, their teaching is classified as part of the vocational sector (2001b). And in such situations the course load is greater as well.

In his 1998 graduating thesis in vocational pedagogy, Bongo has shown a way of transcending the contradictions between workshop learning, vocational theory, and general theory, between vocational teachers and general teachers. He followed a group of carpentry students at an adult education centre for a period of one year. Here the teachers of Norwegian, English, mathematics, and physics grounded themselves in workshop learning and prepared their teaching on the basis of workplace practice. They integrated academic subjects into the actual vocational reality, and the learners learned Norwegian, English, mathematics, and physics from practice to theory. This laid the basis for learning and meaning in a holistic context. Similar experiments are being undertaken at present in vocational courses of study right across the country. Moreover, one might ask oneself if there is a greater freedom to experiment in an adult education institution than in the upper secondary school system with its current academic pressure for examinations and grading. The evaluations of *Reform 94* point out these dilemmas and describe a variety of inventiveness and willingness among all the teachers in the vocational line to help find solutions (Olsen et al. 1998b).

But *Reform 94* is also a step forward. The reform has made vocational studies conspicuous in a new way. It has made working life into an arena of learning and put apprenticeship statutes back on the current agenda. More than two hundred trades and occupations are now recognized by law as eligible for apprenticeship in working life, and new areas are constantly coming into being. Still, the contradictions are far from having been solved in the course of the latest development in vocational education in Norway. The extension of schooling to two years of vocational classes before entering apprenticeship and the limitation of the possibilities of entering apprenticeships directly after compulsory education might have increased the difficulties for working class youth in the difficult transition from school to work. I will return to this matter in the concluding chapter.

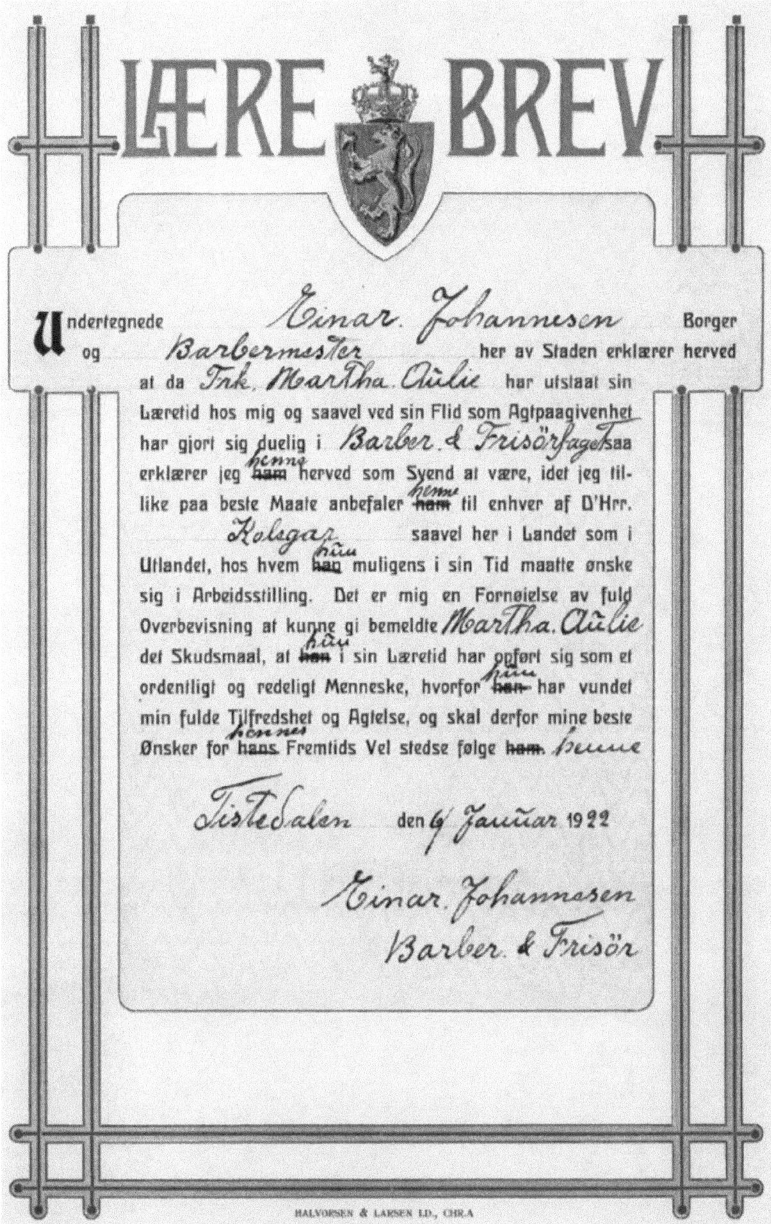
LÆRE BREV

Undertegnede Einar Johannesen Borger og Barbermester her av Staden erklærer herved at da Frk. Martha Aulie har utstaat sin Læretid hos mig og saavel ved sin Flid som Agtpaagivenhet har gjort sig duelig i Barber & Frisörfaget saa erklærer jeg ~~ham~~ henne herved som Svend at være, idet jeg tillike paa beste Maate anbefaler ~~ham~~ henne til enhver af D'Hrr. Kolegaer saavel her i Landet som i Utlandet, hos hvem ~~han~~ hun muligens i sin Tid maatte ønske sig i Arbeidsstilling. Det er mig en Fornøielse av fuld Overbevisning at kunne gi bemeldte Martha Aulie det Skudsmaal, at ~~han~~ hun i sin Læretid har opført sig som et ordentligt og redeligt Menneske, hvorfor ~~han~~ hun har vundet min fulde Tilfredshet og Agtelse, og skal derfor mine beste Ønsker for ~~hans~~ hennes Fremtids Vel stedse følge ~~ham~~ henne

Tistedalen den 6 Januar 1922

Einar Johannesen
Barber & Frisör

HALVORSEN & LARSEN LD., CHR.A

Figure 6: Apprenticeship certificate for a hairdressing apprentice of 1922.

CHAPTER 5

# Working Life as a Learning Arena

Two important themes in the debate about how we learn and how we teach are working life as an arena for learning, and research into work-based learning. Now, after a very long period of strong support for school-desk learning and its extension and development, people have begun to pose critical questions about this process. Various alternative forms of learning are very much part of the discourse today. Nowadays, working knowledge, productive learning on the job, situated learning, master-teacher learning, and master-apprenticeship learning are all central concepts in educational discourse (Billett 2000; Boud&Symes 2000; Coy 1989; Lave&Wenger 1991; Kvale 1993; Nielsen&Kvale 1999). A perspective developed by Lennart Nilsson (1986, 1992), and which is important in this connection, is that now as never before there is access to fundamental, operative, adaptable, vocational didactic knowledge for advancing vocational learning and the development of vocational identity (see also Roldan 2001). In addition, this means that we have a greater understanding of how the human being learns through activity.

At the same time, within this field there is a rich comparative tradition of research into working life. The relationship between those competences the labour force needs in working life and the development of these competences in the individual worker in production has been a subject of debate from the inception of industrialism and on up to the present. Relations between learning at school, learning in the workplace, general education, vocational education, and the various learning traditions are important the world over, despite the fact that there are great variations in the way different countries have built up their industrial production.

The American tradition, for instance, has been to eliminate as much 'mental work' as possible from the shop floor; European traditions have kept more vocationally qualified work on the factory floor (Mjelde 1986, Castro&Carvalho 1985).

European comparative empirical research into industrial development and the growth of the division of labour contribute to an understanding of the complex nature of these phenomena. One good example of such research is Maurice and Sellier's (1979) work on the development of educational systems and the organization of labour in Germany and France. In Germany, the apprenticeship system was adapted to industrialization through the close co-operation of the interests of the state, industry, the school system, and the crafts sector. In a well-regulated system of combined practical and theoretical training, the students work to receive their craft certificates. Sixty per cent of the youth go through such educational processes (Heinz 2001). This qualifies them for further education at the college level. In France by comparison, the hours spent learning often do not result in a craft certificate, and moreover, there is a deep split between intellectual and manual work. Engineers, for example, get a large part of their education at special *grandes écoles* far from the workshop floor.

In Brazil and Argentina, the development of a large public vocational educational system in the schools has resulted in the production of qualified skilled workers. However, the Brazilian engineering colleges have used the French college system as their model, and researchers find that the technical schools of Brazil emphasize theory while offering very little hands-on experience. The consequent gulf between the skilled workforce and the engineers is a barrier to communication. As the researchers Claudio de Moura Castro and Ruy de Quadros Carvalho concluded about this problem, 'The marriage of abstraction with grease has been the most vulnerable spot in the Brazilian technical and vocational education' (1985, 26).

Both in Brazil and in Norway, one finds the opposition between intellectual and manual labour, between the vocational and general education branches of study in general, and between the two paths to education specifically – one for the worker, and one for the engineer – and one also finds the complications this creates for the work process. At the industrial firm described in my Apprenticeship Study 1982–84, an apprentice went to the foreman with a set of blueprints and asked 'What am I supposed to do? I can't use this drawing in relation to the machine. The figures don't add up.' The foreman asked him to translate the figures on the drawing to the language that the worker had learned. The foreman explained that they had had to do this with all the blueprints that came from the engineering office. The engineers were not practiced in the use of the lathe and the actual work operations. Their 'theoretical' drawings had to be translated to 'practice' (Mjelde 1993). The engineers were not schooled in production with its actual specifications and terminology. This is one side of the development of the division of labour that is now being questioned.

Research on work-based learning is clearly interdisciplinary. Important contributions have been made by different social science disciplines, by technically-oriented and critical natural science circles, and by research into consciousness and the brain (Damasio 1999; Dreyfus&Dreyfus 1986; Enkenberg 1994 Flyvberg 1991; Schøn 1983). There are many and various dimensions to this research, but they have one thing in common – something that I find very interesting. This is the understanding that human thinking and learning is a holistic process of knowledge acquisition that develops within a social and cultural milieu, rather than being simply a product of the internal functioning of the brain (see Chapter 4).[42] This opens the way to informal and natural workplaces being viewed as a fundamental part of rich learning experience. Learning in the course of working and through apprenticeship schemes is now gaining attention. Researchers are now treating hairdressing salons, construction sites, mines, and restaurants as important learning arenas (Billett 2000; Harris et al.1998).[43]

42 This seems self-evident to me, but following many years' experience with various interpretations of what learning is, and the school's understanding of learning, I find it necessary to emphasize the distinction that is made here.

43 In Sweden and Norway we have had strong traditions of research into working life since World War II. The Working Life Centre in Stockholm and the Work Research Institute in Oslo have been central institutions that have had projects on learning in the workplace. However, these circles seem to have been weakened in recent years by the public sector's lack of willingness to finance such research.

## Traditions of the Workplace as a Learning Arena in Vocational Education

In relation to crafts and industry, the workplace as a learning arena has a long tradition in vocational education. The relationship between practical working life and the vocational school has been crucial for the development of vocational education in the school system. In Norway, the dual system with its combination of vocational trades taught in workshops with subsequent apprenticeships has been a major model in vocational education right from the beginning of school-based vocational education in 1910 (see Chapter 2). School workshops are the major arenas of learning in vocational education. The goal has been that this workshop learning should resemble job conditions in daily working life so far as this is possible. Before the 1974 *Act on Upper Secondary Education* came into effect, the main employer and employee organizations (the main actors in working life) were represented in the commissions of the various trades and on school committees.

The vocational teacher is a central person in the school's workshops, and was so as well under the old vocational education system.[44] The vocational teacher functions more as a foreman of the work, or a master journeyman, than as a traditional teacher. He or she usually has responsibility for all the classes in work techniques and vocational theory, and often for the general or academic subjects as well. Frequently these teachers have the students for many continuous hours

44 I am not certain what I should use here. It is difficult to discuss when workshop learning has been so reduced that the vocational teacher has disappeared from the role of the steady master she/he was in the old vocational school. Researchers evaluating *Reform 94* have not managed to bring forward the existence of the workshop in the schools. Haga&Michelsen (1993) introduce the concept 'trade principle' versus 'course principle' in relation to the various learning activities that they have found in the vocational schools. However, I believe that these concepts are not very useful for understanding the different learning arenas which are particularly characteristic of vocational schools, and which are most obvious when one goes into the branch of study where one finds the vocational trades in the secondary school system.

every week. The way the vocational teachers have obtained their competence as teachers is that they are first schooled as skilled workers in the crafts or trades before they begin to teach. So they make a very heterogeneous group with craft certificates, trade certificates, or vocational education acquired on labour market, a location where the only constant is change. Most of them have taken pedagogical education while they were actually working as teachers. However, a common criterion is precisely the fact that the teachers have a double armature: they are employed as teachers within the school while at the same time retaining close ties to the working life where they have practiced their crafts and vocations. From their experiences with the labour market, they have acquired the norms and values they practice in their work as teachers. These norms and values, albeit with great variation, are partly recognizable in the school-based vocational workshops. Every vocation has its special characteristics, its form of technical or vocational expression, and its language and social form, and is characterized by traditions derived from the history of the crafts and industry sector. Tailoring and auto mechanics have the characteristics of masculine vocations in Norway, yet each has its different traditions, while dressmaking and the needle trades are women-dominated. Newer vocations in the service sector seem to be marked by the women-dominated traditions of home economics and nursing, or what is referred to as the caring professions.

At first glance, the forms of communication between teacher and pupil in the workshops could seem authoritarian in the old, traditional vocation education. This was most evident in trades with one-year workshop schooling, when the pupils had to depend on employment at only a few workplaces after they had finished with school. (The teachers had strong relations to their trades, and employers contacted the teachers in order to get 'good' apprentices. The teachers' recommendations counted and were influential in relation to whether students found apprenticeship places.) At first sight, communication forms can seem authoritarian and directly oppressive to the student. In an open workshop location the teacher supervises every step the pupil takes and gives praise and criticism openly in the group setting, often in a direct and public way. Vocational teachers believe that this is their job. They refer directly to external norms, to the norms of 'real working life'. A typical assertion is, 'How will things go for this lad if I don't teach him to behave himself properly? He should be here at eight o'clock in the morning, not five after. What will happen to him if I don't teach him to be precise? I have to teach him to be punctual; they won't put up with such nonsense at the workplace. If he's not punctual, he won't last long in a job' (Lesjö 1979, Mjelde 1987).

Haga and Michelsen's investigation into vocational teachers' work consciousness shows that these teachers feel a strong ambivalence about the conflict between the norms and values they acquired earlier from their workplaces in the crafts, industry, and service sectors, and the world they encounter in the schools (1993).[45] What constitutes a good vocational teacher? It seems that the image of the skilled tradesman predominates here. As one of those interviewed put it:

> You're continually running into new things. Saying that someone has finished and graduated – that I take as a bad sign. Sure, you can work yourself up to a comfortable level, and plough on using what you used last year, but there is always a need to adapt yourself, especially in relation to the students you have. What went down last year won't go down next year. You always have to be adjusting yourself. And new things crop up that you feel motivated for, and that are interesting for your trade, so there is always something more that you want to pass on to the student (Haga&Michelsen, 1993).

Thus, a desirable teacher is a specialist in a trade who knows the trade, follows its ongoing development with interest, and is able to communicate these developments in a positive way. But what about a person who is both a specialist and a pedagogue? On one hand, such a person is marked by the norms associated with the working life of a well skilled tradesperson and his or her practical work. On the other hand, it is evident that vocational teaching is above all a pedagogical profes-

45 Speaking generally about vocational teachers in all their diversity, who work in vocational programmes, I find that the empirical material here is rather meagre, but this study is one of the few in the field and is therefore important. The data base has been drawn from three secondary schools in Vestland on the west coast of Norway, from interviews conducted with teachers in the metal trades. There are research tasks here that are still waiting to be taken up.

sion. Both features are components of the vocational teacher's self-realization. But this study also shows that there was variation within the group studied. The researchers found different interpretations of how the teaching ought preferably to be shaped. Some teachers said it was appropriate to organize the instruction in such a way that the working life norms and values were integrated and included in the teaching fundamentals to as great a degree as possible. These teachers aimed to approximate the structural contours of working processes between teaching in school and training on the job in a firm. For them, the actual trade or vocation occupies the central position. The more pedagogically oriented teachers rejected 'production pedagogy' as a proper direction for shaping the teaching. 'The teacher vocation' was converted to 'learning principles' and the profession-oriented products of labour and learning were subordinated to the learning process.

Vocational teachers frequently maintain contact with their former workplaces after they have moved on to teaching positions in the school system. Haga and Michelsen also show in their study that the 'skilled worker' teacher frequently longs for her/his vocation and working life. One of those interviewed put is as follows:

> And beyond that, I personally, myself, have accordingly very good contact with firm NN. In fact, I work there every summer. They ring me up before the summer holidays, and they need help then...in summer. And I really appreciate it. And this even though it's seven years since I left NN. And they continue to call me every summer, which I find very positive. Yeah, not only that, but it's really rewarding for me, myself. Finally to be really creative, myself. Just to do ... have the feeling of doing something, some work with your hands, but don't get me wrong. There is more than enough work involved in teaching these students here too, but really to get to see something again of the concrete stuff I work with. That's really good for the way I feel, myself. (1993, 39)

The study shows a variation on this question, but these connections mean that vocational teachers are often actively involved in finding and recommending apprenticeship positions for their students when these students finish their basic courses.

These issues present other dilemmas as well. The 'master tradesperson' orientation represents qualities that are often stressed in the professional and public rhetoric. The vocational expert is a valuable connection with working life, and is often the first to communicate the system of norms of working life. As such, her/his non-academic ways can be a welcome change for school-weary pupils. But this may not always be a good thing. Trained in the role of apprentice, the master often demands in a dictatorial way the complete submission of his or her apprentices – just as the guilds of the Middle Ages were full of secret arrangements, generational strife, and power struggles (Liljeström 1979, Mjelde 1990a&b). She/he may be a victim of a tradition of very asymmetrical power relationships in which instruction is by command and not by explanation. Instruction can be viewed as much in line with the ways that knowledge is shown and learned in practice in 'craftwork', but pupils/apprentices may respond poorly to instructions perceived as callous orders. On construction sites, for example, the blueprints are considered the teacher's or masters 'private property', and she/he keeps them away from the apprentices/students, all the while commanding them to 'Do this! Nail up that plank! Mix that plaster!' The student/apprentice may get no explanation about why things should be done in such and such a manner. From this system of norms, what can stand out as problematic is the development of a didactic for abstract and theoretical understanding.

Thus, vocational teachers also carry along in their luggage a split learning tradition. On one hand, they themselves have learned in the master-apprenticeship tradition, the good sides of which are the relational understanding of learning through activity. On the other hand, this tradition is marked by the split between the different worlds of practical work, vocational theory, the traditional classroom learning, and vocational didactics 'What?', 'How?' and 'Why?' The foundations of the master-teacher's thinking provide no basis for romanticism, either from the historical or the present-day perspective. What I am talking about here is the vocational didactic learning model we can see in the reality of learning through activity. This activity learning is carried out in conjunction with others, and that social act can often contribute to the better organization of learning situations in general.

The proficiency of craft skills must be learned through practice, but the organization of these learning processes must also include words and explanations. Carpentry teacher and master's student Hans

Bjelke says that one of the dilemmas is that despite the fact that working together is an important element in vocational learning, the everyday language register plays a limiting role. The lack of language elaboration, of verbal explanation, is advanced to an excessive degree as something positive.

These are dilemmas that mark both vocational fields of study and vocational teacher education. It is these dilemmas that have produced the theoretical impoverishment of vocational education in the past century, and this is the case whether one speaks of masonry, plumbing, hairdressing, or nursing.

## Apprentices' Experiences in Working and Learning

Many different methods have been used to organize learning at the point where school intersects with working life, through the development of vocational education within the school system (see Chapter 2). In vocational trades such as tool-making that had developed full skills instruction through the schools, it was common to place the students out in enterprises in the course of the school year. In other vocations, such as the needle trades and the radio and electronics field that also had full instruction within the school system, all the way to the level of the craft certificate, this out-placement tradition was lacking. Before *Reform 94* there was great variation within the vocational trades. It is possible that the reform has led to more homogeneity with the enactment of 'two years of schooling, and two years in working life'. But differences remain in the way this is carried out. There is also a great diversity in the vocational sector in relation to life in the firm or enterprise.

## Apprenticing

As I have said, in Europe 'apprenticing' has a long tradition with roots in the days of the guilds. In the form of a covenant, apprentices placed their labour power at the disposition of a master craftsman in return for room and board, often for many years. This could prove to be a 'merciless' situation. The apprentices and journeyman were completely at the mercy of the master who had complete control over their lives. In modern times apprenticeship schemes have been regulated by legislation. In Norway, the 1980 *Act on Education in Working Life* regulated the rights and duties of both the firms and the apprentices. Enterprises that take in apprentices must be approved as 'teaching firms'. A vocationally qualified person must be appointed to look after the firm's apprenticeships. The enterprise is supposed to acquaint the apprentice with the apprenticeship plan and the specifications for taking the craft or journeyman examinations. The firm also has to give the apprentice the necessary training and experience to reach the stipulated goal. The provisions also include rules that require the firm to enrol the apprentices in relevant courses in the school system and to allow them to attend these without loss of wages. The law has provisions for making sure that the apprentices' rights are respected. But laws and provisions are one thing, and reality can be quite another matter.

In the *Apprenticeship Study 1982–84*, most apprentices expressed satisfaction with obtaining an apprenticeship. When one expresses satisfaction with a situation, it is done in relation to something else. Most of the apprentices in the study (1,438 of 1,617 studied) still preferred to learn at the workplace rather than at the school. They experienced the apprenticeship situation as better in the extreme than the school situation, but this does not mean that their apprenticeship experiences were unproblematic. One hundred apprentices in the study found the apprenticeship situation so difficult that they now would prefer to have taken their instruction through the school system. It was particularly the girls in the commerce and service vocations who wished they had stayed in school until they took their craft examination. One hairdressing apprentice said:

> You get used. You do all the work of a qualified hairdresser, but you're paid much worse. The employer knows too little about the laws. To get the necessary training I had to fight with the master for six months. If you go to school every day you're guaranteed full instruction. In the salon it's easy to be put into another agenda' (Mjelde 1993,102).

This hairdressing apprentice had had to fight for her right to participate in the apprenticeship school programme once a week, a right with which the master was duty-bound to comply. The field of hairdressing seems to be marked by small workplaces, even in the chains, where one works closely together with others. The master and apprentice may be the only two in the salon, but every salon has its own specific characteristics. Stephen Billett's empirical work from research into hairdressing salons in Australia shows the range of variation (2000, 9). There are both similarities and differences between how the apprentices solve the work operations in the various hairdressing salons. The size of the hairdressing salon, the number of employees, its position, and its clientele were determining factors related to the way the learning situation developed.

The world of trade and commerce is also marked by small workplaces with close work relations. As one cook said in my apprenticeship study:

> I would prefer going to school. I was too old to become an apprentice, to find myself in all those shit jobs. The basic attitude seemed to be, 'My apprenticeship period was totally shitty, so yours is going to be the same.' This was said to me by one and all of the cooks at my place of work (Mjelde 1993, 102).

This apprentice pointed out that he was given the work that the others wanted to avoid, and that he was too old for that. Normally apprentices go out into firms right after their basic schooling or after one year at a workshop school. My apprenticeship study revealed a considerable spread of age among those who were in the third year of apprenticeship: 60 per cent were between sixteen and twenty, and 40 per cent were between twenty and twenty-five. The apprentice cited above was twenty-four.

The apprentices in the study were not very clear about the supervisory regulations, and only 35 per cent of the supervisory personnel had made contact with the apprentice. Every workplace has its own culture, and the different trades and vocations have their own traditions that distinguish the workplaces. But they have one thing in common, namely that they are production firms, where the leading factors are the press of time and economy. One of the apprentices from graphics expressed this as follows: 'The employer doesn't have time to teach us on the job. We get the message that we are not there to learn. The meaning we get is that we ought to learn at school'. According to Flaaten 1999, Henri Werring, in his book called *Læring i arbeidslivet* [Learning at Work] points out that there is a contradictory relationship between the interests of production and those of learning:

> The primary task of working life is not to educate people. A firm does not have the same main task as that of a school. The main task of a firm is and will always be to take care of its creation of value as a necessity for maintaining a certain standard of living. Other activities like, for example, learning, are activities that must be viewed in relation to the creation of value, hence in relation to qualifying the further creation of value (Werring 1982, cited in Flaaten 1999 page 3).

Another factor that makes learning in the manual labour market problematic can be work that is marked by routine. A tinsmith/sheet-metal worker said, 'You get so many dirty jobs as an apprentice. There's too much routine and stress.' Egil Midtlyng shows that large parts of working hours in the building and installation trades are used for monotonous work (1998). Another point of view on this question is found in Sandra Val Flaatten, who did her thesis on apprenticeship training at Norsk Hydro. She found that electrical and process operator apprentices felt that they had gone from a content-rich 'everyday life of learning', to a normal life of 'everyday work'. After a while the work became routine (1999, 129). In the Apprenticeship Study 1982–84, 36 per cent of the apprentices were in contract work, and 83 per cent of these were in the building and installation branch. One electrical apprentice said, 'The down side is that when an apprentice works by contract it is easier for him to be put at the same job for a long time. Because he can do that quickly, then the contract comes off well' (Mjelde 1993, 143). Another aspect was stressed by a carpentry apprentice: 'Contract work goes so fast that there's a lot of sloppy work, and that shouldn't happen, not when apprentices are supposed to take up that same work. So then the quality of the work goes down' (p. 144).

Nevertheless, despite the problems with on-the-job training, contract work, and work characterized by routine, apprentices preferred the learning situation on the job to what they had known at school. This finding is pregnant with contradictions, and studies show how difficult it is to combine and reconcile value-creation with apprentice training on the manual labour market. However, these questions are now understood and placed on the agenda to a greater degree than they were earlier. *Reform 94* is an important contributing factor in this direction.

And if nothing else, the apprentice can take comfort from the perspective of time. Apprenticeship has time limits. This period of life is considered by the apprentices to be a time of transition. Today, as before *Reform 94* (see also Flaatten 1999), the length of the apprenticeship depends upon the trade or profession, but the apprentice knows that this period has a definite end, and knowing that, one can put up with a lot (Mjelde 1988b, 142).

## Reform 94 and the Workplace as Learning Arena

These reforms have put 'the workplace as learning arena' and the apprenticeship scheme on the public agenda. One of the issues at the leading edge of *Reform 94* was the desire that the scholarly aspect of vocational education be strengthened, and that the enterprises that accepted apprentices should take greater responsibility than they did earlier for the training component (Sakslind 1985, 5). Ole Johnny Olsen maintains that the reform involves a public expectation that the firms take on the role of learning institution to a much greater degree than earlier, in the formation of the apprentice's personal as well as vocational life (1998, 2).

What is qualitatively new in *Reform 94* is the demand for the structuring of the apprentice's learning situation in the firm. The first year is to be 'learning time' for the apprentice; the second should be a year of creating value. In reality this division as such probably would not suit most apprentices' everyday lives, and will vary from one vocation to the next. In some fields the apprentice can be productive from the beginning; in others, good training situations are required before the apprentice can contribute to production. What is new is that there are expectations that training within the firm is now planned, structured, and evaluated to a greater extent than before. The apprentice is supposed to have someone available at the workplace that has been given the responsibility to see that the learning process functions satisfactorily. The training of those responsible for the firm's apprenticeship programmes is also part of this work. Mentor schemes are being instituted.

Another aspect of the reform is the new expectation that the school system and working life co-operate. This is actually back to the way it worked before the 1974 *Act on Upper Secondary Education*, which integrated vocational and academic education under one law. Now Labour and Capital are back in the arena of vocational education. Co-operation between the vocational fields within the schools and with working life – between vocational teachers and the enterprises – is being raised and legitimized. With *Reform 94*, the apprenticeship scheme has been expanded into new fields that have few experiences with apprenticeships. The service sector and professions have built out the apprenticeship system following the trajectory of the expanding labour market (see Chapter 7).

Learning in a classroom tradition and learning on the job have encountered new challenges in the vocational education of the crafts and industry sector, as has been the case in higher education. The development of the 'educational society' in the past thirty years, with the strong faith in the alpha and the omega of school-based learning, has created a distance between school and working life beside which a question mark has now been placed. In 1985 Rune Sakslind pointed out that one of the major problems with the educational system that was built up following the Second World War is that it continues to advance a theory-based tradition of knowledge that is miles away from the world of work (Sakslind 1985, 2). This has happened in higher education as well as at the level of the basic comprehensive school, and in the creation of the secondary comprehensive school system with its attempts at integration between academic collegiate school and vocational education for crafts and industry.

We also find the same phenomena and contradictions in other profession-directed forms of education. Nursing education has gone from a system based on 'apprenticeship schemes' in a hospital thirty years ago, to theory-oriented classroom instruction at the colleges and universities. The apprentice situation in the hospitals was marked by a silent master-apprentice model with little verbal communication and explanation (Prestbakmo 1997). Ragnhild Prestbakmo says that in her investigation of the course of studies for nursing, practical instruction was marked by a master-apprentice relationship wherein the master did not have the time to instruct her/his apprentice (1997, 4). But the theory-oriented classroom teaching that has developed seems to have led to a 'praxis shock' for the graduating nurses (Sandvik 1997). This development is full of contradictions. Another point put forward by Prestbakmo is that at the same time when the argument is advanced for apprenticeship learning, there is in fact a cutting back of the practicum component of training in the field of nursing, with a corresponding increase in the theoretical component (2001, 10).

The contradictions between various learning arenas are just as real in the education of medical doctors or engineers as they are in the training of teachers or nurses. New questions are put on the agenda, but as we have seen, there is no basis for idealizing work-based learning and apprenticeship schemes. We must look critically both at learning in the educational institutions and on-the-job learning, and we must try to advance our understanding and organization of good learning in both places.

Figure 7: Vocational training – on the job or in educational institutions?

# Part Two

# Gender and Skills in Vocational Education

CHAPTER 6

# Dinner through Text: A Social History of How Home Economics Teaching Entered the School System

## Home Economics and the Era of Scientific Optimism

With the onset of industrialization in Norway, together with the development of the nuclear family and the expansion of the common public school system at the close of the nineteenth century, Norway saw the development of school kitchens and instruction in cooking and nutrition. This led to the need for relevant manuals. In this chapter I examine Norway's first textbook in home economics. The first textbook in home economics for the compulsory school system first saw the light of day in 1891. *Kogebok for folkeskolen og hjemmet (Cookbook for School and Home)* was written by Dorothea Christensen and published by the J. W. Cappelen publishing house in Kristiania.[46] The price was 'in soft cover, 45 *øre*, and in soft red cloth cover, 50 *øre*'.[47] Dorothea Christensen was determined that every child should be able to have a cookbook that included 'a selection of dishes in rather small portions and as far as possible precise statements of quantities and weights', as she put it in the book's Foreword. The *Cookbook for School and Home* came out in an edited version in 1894, and on that occasion it was co-authored by Helga Helgesen. The 1894 edition appeared with amendments and enlargements. This edition of the book was self-published, with the aim that this might make it more cheaply available. The largest possible number of Norwegians ought to be able to own it. The authors were determined

46 See supra note 5, Chapter 2.
47 100 øre = 1 krone (crown). Today 6-7 kroner = $1.00.

that the book should be widely disseminated and put to use in thousands of homes. As they said in the foreword: 'The book is not simply to be thought a school book. It has also been prepared with its specific purpose being the many very modest homes, where cookbooks have never been utilized, or where a proper general cookbook has never been employed for such a book is too lavish for their humble means.'[48]

Faith in mass enlightenment and schooling for the whole populace as a solution to the problems of poverty was very much part of the social thinking of the era. The school statutes of 1860 and 1889 were linked to a development that moved away from the itinerant school, which had Christian knowledge as its predominant goal, and towards permanent schools espousing 'secular knowledge'. A law requiring seven years of compulsory schooling was inaugurated and rules were established about how many weeks school should be conducted in the course of the year. The writer and scientist Peter Christen Asbjørnsen published his cookbook, *Sensible Cookery,* under the pseudonym Clemens Bonifacius in 1864 (cited in Wærness 1991) He was concerned that women's lack of skills in food preparation inflicted great losses on the country. He did his bit to urge that the general schools take up instruction in food and cooking. The solution, according to Asbjørnsen, was that 'by means of theoretical learning at school the basis must be laid for women to become better housewives'.

Another perspective advanced during this period was the relationship between science and domestic science (Helgesen 1914, 1928, Wærness 1991). One person of influence who had made this connection long before was the English seventeenth century scholar and statesman Francis Bacon (Portelli 1996, 18). *The Chemistry of Cooking and Housekeeping*, by the German Dr. Klencke, was published in Norwegian in 1859 (in Wærness 1991). The introduction to this volume maintained that it was important to introduce knowledge of science to the kitchen and to housekeeping. Thus it was that the *Cookbook for School and Home* took up this challenge in the

48 The cited passages from the cookery book have been translated into English for use in this chapter.

1890s. The state chemist Ludvig Henrik Benjamin Schmelck had gone over the book. This co-operative effort was part of the scientific optimism of the era, and the connection to the natural sciences was clear. This alliance has continued to colour the development of domestic science, or home economics, up to the present (see also Ulltveit 1990, 60). Even in this worthy project there was a gender division of labour. The natural science themes were taught by men in separate classrooms far away from the bustle of the kitchen where the practical instruction was given by women.

Another aspect of this theme has been illuminated by the doctoral work of Marianne Holck (2001). Holck analysed the chemistry that was used as a support subject in higher professional education, paying special attention to vocational teacher training in the nutritional, health, and environmental fields. She pointed out that this education has been criticized abroad for having been only minimally connected to practical situations and for being stuffed with traditional professional material. She found that the same criticism remains applicable to Norwegian education today.

## Norway the Poor, Anno 1890

Ottar Brox writes in an article in *Samtiden* that 'Norway was an underdeveloped country in 1890, with a national product of the same magnitude as a small, poor underdeveloped country' (1990). For the general populace there was neither much school-going nor much food. 'One takes 12 eggs and cream,' wrote Hanna Winsnes 'but,' commented the poor of Norway with sarcasm, as they did in England, 'no one says where you can take them from.' England's Hanna Winsnes was Mrs. Beaton, and England too had problems with a rate of poverty that grew expansively with the onset of industrialism. The historian Anna Davin has shown that one problem in Britain was that the working class in the nineteenth century was not reproducing itself (1982; see also Portelli 1996). There was not enough labour power for the factories. The common people were dying of under-nourishment and sickness. Hygiene and nutrition were big problems, something that Gudrun Ulltveit in her analysis of nineteenth century cookbooks shows to have been common to Norway as well (1990). These problems inspired women of the affluent classes to become engaged in the struggle for domestic science education for the benefit of the developing working class.

## Two Pioneer Women: Dorothea von der Lippe Christensen and Helga Bernadine Helgesen

Housewife ideology blossomed in the climate of the day and the science of housekeeping developed in Norway as in England. How was housework carried out in 1891? According to the historian Kari Melby, there is very little concrete historical knowledge about the development of housework (1985, 207). The everyday life of ordinary people, and particularly, women's everyday life, seldom achieved mention in the grand historical narratives. Housework has continued to be women's work and is still not part of hegemonic academic thinking. The ongoing production of labour power – its daily rejuvenation and generational replacement is missing. And we know comparatively little about the ideology that has encompassed this work and those who have carried it out in different times in history. In his work *A Millennium of Family Change*, Wally Seccombe writes: 'The exclusion of labour-power's daily and generational reproduction from the conception of modes of production has made it almost impossible to see families as labour teams, pumping the blood through socio-economic systems' (1995, 11).

The field of women's studies has placed these themes on the agenda in recent decades. Ann Oakley has written in her epoch-making *The Sociology of Housework* about how she documented, and placed question marks on the traditional division of labour on the domestic front. The woman's role in this unpaid production has been central to this debate (1974). Women have been responsible for the labour of caring for family members, conducting housework, and providing personal services (Ve 1999, 28). Critical women researchers have been applying question marks to what this has done to men's actions and ways of thinking.

How this gender division arose and became part of our school system can be comprehended by, among other things, an analysis of the dominating gender ideology in society, especially with regard to late nineteenth-century judgements about what was men's work and what was women's work. Dorothea Christensen cites her grandfather in an article 'From a Mother to Mothers' which she wrote in 1887[49]:

> When, twenty-five years ago I had stuffed my Head with all of Today's kaleidoscopic Knowledge, and was proudly wandering around with my Books under my arm, with the sweet Consciousness that I knew 4 Languages, Physics, Chemistry, Astronomy, Literature, Mythology, Mathematics, and a whole Number of other Things, while, from my lofty intellectual Stance, I basically had nothing but Scorn for the Care of the House and physical Work, and my Grandfather shook his white Head at me and my learned Girlfriends, and he said, 'Dear Child, Your upbringing is completely crazy. You are learning nothing about what you will in all likelihood become, a poor Man's Housewife.' We listened to Grandfather's obsolete nonsense and smiled haughtily.

Dorothea Christensen's grandfather was completely in tune with the dominant thinking of the day, and with the contradictions that we know from the gender debate, a debate that continues today, more than a century later (see Mjelde 2004). One group of male social scientists, whose members were referred to as 'domestic feminists', looked on women primarily as sexual vessels. Biology was the fate of women. These men believed that women could improve their social status and increase their value in society by being more skilled in their traditional sphere of activity (Strauss 1982). More or less this same line of thinking was advanced at various times throughout the twentieth century. But the most highly cultivated form of this thinking was found in the national socialism of Germany with its idolizing of

49 Rector Inger Johanne Nossum at Akershus University College gave me a copy of what seems to be a machine-written copy of this original document dating from 1887. Gudrun Ulltveit (1990) refers to an article by Dorothea Christensen with the same title, but published in *Bergens Aftenblad* in 1889.

women's place with the slogan 'kinder, kirche, küche' (Bridenthal, Grossmann&Kaplan 1984). Women's place was with the children, in the church, and the kitchen. Of course, these are assumptions which remain all too alive and well today, especially in the research tradition of socio-biology and in conservative social and political circles (Fukuyama 1997).

Dorothea Christensen, née Frost (1849–1909) took her ideas from various sources. She was the well-educated and well-travelled daughter of a Lutheran priest and received the best education available to women of that time. She attended Nissen School in Kristiania where she sat for the governess examination (Parelius 1970). In 1871 at the age of twenty-two, she married Julius Christensen, a doctor from Sandefjord. He was the mayor of that city for a number of years, and for two periods he was also an alternative member of parliament. She visited several countries on the continent, including Germany and France. In what she wrote in 1887 she said that she had been surprised to see how the girl child in the large, rich, cultured countries was able to undertake a rather different practical education from what they received in Norway. She described a situation in France:

> I recall that on one occasion down there I entered a large School and saw the Lady Teacher and all the pupils wandering about in lengthy and high-necked Pinafore Smocks (to save their Clothing) while the Teacher demonstrated the different Ways one could prepare Coffee. How many bitter Words from young Husbands and how many secret Tears from young Housewives would have been Spared, if such were also to be done in our Schools. I began to waver considerably in terms of my former Certainty, and when I myself had House and Children, my Doubt grew into Certainty, and I was forced to say with Irritation that School and Upbringing have neglected to provide me with what life strongly demands, and what is demanded of me.

Dorothea Christensen worked in charitable organizations. She founded not only a people's library, but also a weaving studio and a handicrafts centre. In the article 'From a Mother to Mothers' in *Bergens Aftenbladet* in 1889 she came into the light as an advocate for more practical education for young girls, more than was currently available to them in the academic school (see *supra,* note 2). In 1890 she established the first school-based teaching kitchen in the country – in the cellar of the Sandefjord primary school. The first class to go through this course was composed of nine students (Parelius 1970; Eden Johnsen 1986). Miss Margethe Ebbesen cooked and instructed in the kitchen, and Mrs. Christensen wrote about it. Such a clear division between the head and the hands was part of the order of things, although in this instance the division was between women of the same affluent class. At that time, middle-class women were not supposed to take part in practical housework. As we are told in *Skolekjøkkensaken i Norge gjennom 50 år (On the Matter of the School Kitchen in Norway over 50 Years)*: 'Miss Ebbesen was also a lady of society, and it was characteristic of public opinion of the time that practical work, and especially housework, that many thought it odd that she would perform the work of a serving girl' (KUFD 1941, 9). Nor was Dorothea Christensen a stranger to the idea that men ought to take part in housekeeping work. She wrote: 'When house help is not available, the husband and sons must do their share of domestic labour.'

The pioneer Helga Bernadine Helgesen (1863–1936) had had other experiences that were fundamental to her engagement in the development of teaching the arts of housekeeping. She had been born at Hønefoss and grew up on Alme Farm in Norderhov. In 1887 she took her teacher's examination at Nissen's School for Girls in Kristiania, after which she began work as a teacher at Kampen School in 1889. Oluf Melvold (1988) describes Kampen at the end of the nineteenth century as one of the most miserable suburban communities within Aker County (today an upscale part of Oslo's inner city), not only with regard to the low standard of living and hygiene, but also in terms of general conditions. Kampen was also known as the quarter where the brickyard workers lived. It was building activity in Kristiania that laid the basis for jobs for men, women, and children at the end of the nineteenth century. Melvold describes Helga Helgesen as a person richly endowed with social instinct and social consciousness. Out of her encounters with the impoverished working population of Kampen, and especially with the undernourished or badly nourished young, she began to think about how she, as a well-educated person, could help to better the local conditions. She also sought answers abroad. With a travel grant and a research stipend from the Queen Mother Josephine Fund, she journeyed to England in order to look into secondary education there. While in Britain she studied and took her examination at the Glasgow Training School of Cookery for Teachers, which was led by the domestic science pioneer of Scotland, Margaret Black (KUF 1941, 12).[50]

In 1891, experimental instruction in domestic science was started at Kampen School by Helga Helgesen. She considered it very important to teach girls 'household economy'. In 1892 she inaugurated 'the state course for educating lady school teachers in cookery', this also at Kampen. These initiatives became the basis for the State Teachers' College in Home Economics which was established at Stabekk in the western suburbs of Kristiania in 1909. Helga Helgesen wrote innumerable articles, and in 1928 a book on teaching school cookery. In an article dated 1914, she showed that from the 1890s, home economics teaching was directed to both girls and boys. Anna-Clara Eden Johnsen published pictures from Ytre Rendalen Itinerant School that show both boys and girls in full activity in the kitchen (1986). The participation of boys in home economics seems to have varied with the different epochs of schooling. Lorraine Portelli shows that food preparation had been introduced to the teaching of boys in England as early as 1912 (1996, 27). Helga Helgesen corrected and expanded the 1894 cookery/home economics textbook and it remained in use in the primary schools for many years. A revised version with the title *Home Economics* was endorsed for use in the secondary modern schools and folk high schools[51] right into the 1970s.

Dorothea Christensen was sixteen years older than Helga Helgesen, and died on February 28, 1908, at the age of sixty. Helga Helgesen never married; instead, she seems to have devoted her life to the cause of the school kitchen, a cause that she pursued right up to her death in 1936 at the age of seventy-three. Two women of very different destinies thus came forward to found home economics education in Norway. In addition, they produced Norway's first textbook designed for practical application.

50 I have encountered various spellings for Margaret Black's surname – Black, Blacke, Blake. Helga Helgesen however used 'Black' in her original texts.

51 There are eighty-four folk high schools or popular colleges offering non-credit courses in a wide variety of subjects. Most are residential schools and they are located in most parts of Norway.

## The First Textbook Produced for Practical Application

The textbook in the vocational fields occupies a different place in the learning situation than does the textbook in the traditional grammar school (Askerøi&Høie 1999; Berg 1999). In workshop learning, one learns by means of activity. One uses one's hands making things, performing a service, or preparing food. Activity is central and one produces something tangible (Mjelde 1995). Vocational theory is closely linked to its various fields, and the books of vocational theory are where one seeks out such things as recipes, instruction protocols, and practical guidance. For example, one goes to the books to find standards of measurement in the mechanical fields, how one is to combine chemicals when one is about to colour someone's hair, or how to prepare to print something, or one turns to a cookbook to find a recipe. The textbook in home economics is used in close relationship with the co-ordinated work of the hand and the brain. It is a reference work; it lies there; we take a look in it; it gets worn out and splattered. It does not serve simply as a preparatory tool for a written examination.

In his chapter 'The Management of Reality', Per Inge Båtnes discusses various types of learning (1995). In interactive learning one is supposed to put one's hands on or into things, to try things out. This provides familiarity to one's knowledge and it happens in workshop learning in the vocational fields whether one is in a kitchen or in a machine shop. Textbooks are used in different ways in general and vocational education. The pedagogue Leif Langli talks about the limits that textbooks ought to have in a learning process. He says, 'The moment we make a textbook the basis of learning we distance ourselves from the reality of the vocational fields' (personal communication 1995). Does one come to own the knowledge one acquires through 'learning by doing' in a different way from the knowledge gained in the general subjects? It is perhaps interesting to note the division of labour in this project. Dorothea Christensen's 1892 edition of the cookery text was based on the practical work in the first teaching kitchen, but Mrs. Christensen based her writing not on her own practice as a cook or teacher, but rather, it was Miss Ebbesen who cooked and taught, and Mrs. Christensen who observed and wrote (KUF 1941, 63).

## Dinner through Text

The 1894 edition of the cookery textbook is a thin volume of only 110 pages. The major portion is devoted to the preparation of food in general, and dinner in particular. The processes of food preparation have been systematized and written down. They have been transformed into texts to be put into use. The book has a unity and a narrative form with descriptions of milk, eggs, meat, and fish, with emphasis on the nutritional content and with detailed explanations on the subject of preparation. Milk is described as 'one of our most important foodstuffs ... containing salt and water (ca. 87½ %) and casein.'

The pages dealing with economy are conspicuous throughout the whole text. In the section on meat the writers say that 'horsemeat, on the basis of price, is recommended.' With regard to inner organs and blood, detailed descriptions are given from the butchering to the care of the blood to the preparation of the innards. 'A set of entrails costs 3 to 4 crowns and from it one can prepare many good dishes.' In 'Poor man's *foie gras* (ordinary liver fried as though it were from a bird)' the ingredients are given as ½ kilo liver, a little pork, a large spoonful of butter or fat, 1 teaspoon salt, 4 cloves, 1 dl boiling water, 3 dl milk. In the recipe for boiled coffee, it is recommended that the resources be used parsimoniously to the very last drop: '[H]ere one uses 2 dessert spoons of coffee to 1 litre water, plus fish skin for clarification. The coffee ought to boil for 10 minutes, whereupon a teaspoon of dried dandelion blossoms should be added. And one should boil the grounds again, but every third day the grounds must be dealt with, that is, one fills the coffee pot with water and boils it – without adding new coffee – on the basis of the old grounds for a quarter of an hour.' The grounds were at this point discarded and the coffee water could be used to boil up new coffee, and in this way one could 'take a little less coffee' (Melvold 1988, 14).

## The Cookbook as Life-Style Counselling

The *Cookbook for School and Home*, as the title reveals, was not intended only to be thought of as a recipe book for the school kitchen. It was meant to be a form of life counselling. In the foreword to the 1891 edition, Dorothea Christensen wrote: '[S]ince there is seldom a housekeeping book to be found in a working family's home, I have utilized the opportunity, as much as it is my place to admit to such, such that this book is not, strictly speaking, intended to find its home as the cookbook for the school kitchen, so much as it might well come to be used in the child's home.'

The book contains 'Advice for working families of limited means for cheap and nourishing dinner courses.' A menu was provided which would feed 2 adults and 3 children for a year at a total cost of 181.80 crowns. Of the 365 dinner suggestions, a good 120 are based on herring, a further fifty on other fish (coalfish cakes, lutefisk,[52] and stewed cod), and 112 on inner organs as the main ingredient, while only 85 are based on meat (mutton, beef, or pork). The book also contains suggestions for an annual budget, for example, for a family consisting of husband, wife, and two school-age children. The family's total income is estimated at 700.00 crowns per annum (less than $120 at today's rate of exchange). Of this, 96.00 crowns were calculated for house rent, 10.00 for fuel, 70.00 for clothing and footwear, and 10.00 crowns per annum for school supplies. In the foreword, the writers say that Professor Dr. Torup worked out a table for foodstuffs that could be purchased in Kristiania for 10 øre. The cookbooks also recommendations for keeping written accounts: 'Everyone ought diligently to write down how much money they earn or receive and how much they give out in the course of a week. The accounts book is often a good advisor to have.' With full justification this vocation was originally called 'domestic economy', no doubt inspired by the American concept of 'home economics'.[53] The foundation

52 A reconstituted dried cod that has been treated with potash lye.

53 Lorraine Portelli (1996), in 'A Curriculum History of Domestic Subjects in Malta', has an interesting discussion about the name shift in domestic science

stones of the exposition are the natural sciences and economics. Scientific thinking is set up as a means of bettering the general standards of health and to develop people's abilities to live within their means. And this was expected to increase the possibilities of the housewife influencing the morals and the spiritual development of the family. The complete life situation was put on the agenda.

The cookbook also contains detailed 'domestic advice' about such infectious diseases as measles, diphtheria, and cholera, afflictions which were epidemic and often fatal at the end of the nineteenth century. In the event of such diseases one was to act in the following manner: '[A]ll toys, books, and whatever the afflicted has handled ought to be burned, and the sick room is fumigated.' Good advice against physical ills that we are familiar with today was 'anise drops' against the cough and the 'sore throat', '20 drops myrrh in a beer glass filled with water or 1 tsp of potassium chlorate in 2½ dl boiling water, for gargling.' Spirits were only recommended as medicine: 'Spirits do infinitely more damage and ought to only be used as medicine ... Excessive use of beer and spirits leads to sickness, misery, and suffering.'

There is an introduction to the subject of housing – on cleaning, cooking vessels (their nature and use), and the use of fuels, illumination, and water. The description of water has vocational pedagogical dimensions: 'Water is composed of oxygen and hydrogen; it contains dissolved mineral materials and a certain amount of dissolved air. Thus it is we understand how important water is for us, since over half of the weight of our bodies is water.' This is a holistic description with elements of chemistry and physiology. The use of the pronouns 'we', 'us', and 'our' create a whole and immediate understanding of scientific phenomena (Eden Johnsen 1986, Mjelde 1995).

The pedagogical thinkers of the seventeenth century Friedrich Wilhelm August Fröbel and Johann Heinrich Pestalozzi as well as Georg Kershensteiner and the laboratory school principles of John Dewey were part of the educational thinking of the day. Helga Helgesen, at the beginning of her work when she was promoting the

---

teaching in terms of British and American developments. The same type of development has occurred in Norway.

issue of school kitchens, employed arguments from this way of thinking (1928, 196). On the other hand, the cookbook authors write in their foreword to the second edition that since natural science and hygiene are taken up as subjects in the primary school system, they reduced the portion of writing about human nutrition to the smallest possible degree in their book. As we see, this was a development marked by contradictions. The splitting up of subjects and the contradictions between vocational and general education, between workshop learning and classroom learning, and between practical knowledge and theoretical knowledge ran counter to the unitary thinking to which the book's starting point bore witness, and which was the basis for holistic teaching in the school kitchen (Mjelde 1993; 1994a&b). The school kitchen was the kernel of home economics teaching and provided the basis for the development of a complete learning arena.

## The School Kitchen as a Learning Arena

Time and space are of great significance for learning. The school kitchen is an arena for learning by means of one's own activity. One learns by making food. The only picture in the textbook shows the interior of a school kitchen. Young girls in the school's kitchen uniforms carry out different work tasks. The teacher, with pointer in hand, stands at the blackboard where the menu is written. The students read recipes, calculate and weigh ingredients, and use their hands and heads to produce a product. They have to use their general education knowledge and their skills in calculation. Working in the school kitchen, the students learn in the same room over a long period of time. They concentrate on a unified activity, working together for six hours. The classroom model of learning breaks school time into forty-five-minute blocks, and the day is divided up into different subjects. A fundamental question is whether the division of the day into various subjects hinders learning.

Such questions have preoccupied pedagogical thinkers such as John Dewey, Georg Kerschensteiner, Celestin Freinet, and Nadezhda

Krupskaya in the course of the twentieth century (Mjelde 1995, 1996a). Learning by doing, holistic thinking, and the principles of the laboratory schools have been viewed as alternative approaches to organizing teaching and instruction. Anna-Clara Eden Johnsen (1986, 66) cites from *Fifty Years of the School Kitchen Issue* (KUFD 1941): 'The students' own activity has been the solution for our contemporary schools. In the school kitchens the students' own activity has been at work for the past fifty years. Their ability to carry out a task of work on their own, or in common with their comrades has been performed systematically. Their promptness and their ability to combine things have both been sharpened, their sense of solidarity and readiness to help developed.' The home economics textbook of Dorothea Christensen and Helga Helgesen seems to have been laid out according to such unified and holistic thinking.

Anna-Clara Eden Johnsen (1986, 22) [says that the documentary sources of the 1890s show that the pedagogy of the day consistently maintained that home economics teaching were to be supported by the natural sciences and the principles of hygiene. But she also shows that the theoretical portion was gradually left to be performed by the craniums of male teachers, and that the classes in theory were separated temporally and spatially from the lessons in the kitchen. This development resulted in the gradual exclusion of holistic learning, thinking, and collaboration. The germ of this division of labour – the split between the work of the hand and the work of the mind, between women's work and men's work in home economics teaching – is evident in the title of the cookbook, *Cookbook for School and Home*. Even though Dorothea Christensen and Helga Helgesen seem to have been schooled in chemistry, their cookbook was vetted by a man with the title State Chemist Schmelck. Women were the instructors in the schools' kitchen workshops while men taught the theoretical components of natural science and hygiene in classrooms. This was 'the order of things' that has left its mark upon the growth and development of schooling and home economics education right up to the present day (see also Holck 2001).

Figure 8: State school for women home economics teachers at Stabekk, about 1920.

CHAPTER 7

# From Factory and Housework to Oil and Caring: Changes in Girls' Education in the Vocational Fields during the Years of *Reform 94*

The recent decades of expansion of education, in Norway in particular and Scandinavia in general, have witnessed considerable changes in women's opportunities and relations with regard to paid work. Today, women in Norway constitute a majority of those engaged in post-secondary or university and college education. One of the persistent and extensive themes in the fields of women's studies and gender research during the last twenty-year period has been the inquiry into the nature of the conditions that lead to social differences between women and men. Moreover, to at least some degree, the searchlight on these conditions has also been directed to differences between categories of women (Ellingsæter 1995a&b; Ellingsæter et al. 1997; Ellingsæter&Rubery 1997; Gaskell 1995, 59). Has the explosion in education led to new opportunities for women, and generally at the same time, new differences between women? This is a complex question, and we have little thorough empirical knowledge of this subject in relation to developments that have occurred over the past two decades. In this chapter, I want to direct a searchlight on two things: changes and developments in women's work, and the new apprenticeship schemes that are associated with developments in the manual and service sectors of the labour market. These sectors of the labour market have a bearing upon the vocational fields of study in upper secondary education.

In general, the involvement of women in the labour market of Norway has been facilitated by the *Law on Equality between the Sexes*, which came into effect in 1978; this statute established gender quotas and an equality commission. Women's right to education and work at the same pay scales as those of men seem now to be a matter of course.[54] Shifts in the labour market in recent decades have thoroughly reflected these changes, paralleling the politics of the family, which also have been in a state of flux. In addition, Norway has had its Royal Commission which among other things addressed the male role in society, and since this commission, the man's participation in housework and child-rearing has been very much on the agenda.[55]

For the time being in the Western industrialized nations, we seem to be in a transition from an industrially-dominant economy to one dominated by the service sector. In the period between 1972 and 1992, the number employed in industry in Norway fell by almost 100,000, while the number employed in the social and personal services sector rose by over 350,000. Technology has made formerly manual work redundant in many industrial departments, or else whole industries have been 'exported' to places where the labour power is cheaper. The only constant is change. New industries are arising, and they require increasingly more highly qualified labour power. Men have lost industrial jobs, and women have swollen the ranks of the service

54 I am writing this provisionally with full awareness that this is an arena composed of different ideologies contending over questions such as women's place in society, and the condition and importance of the nuclear family. At the time this chapter was originally written, the sitting Minister of Children and Family Affairs, from the Christian People's Party in Norway's coalition government, had instituted a state-financed cash support system for families not using the day-care system; that is to say, these families receive a monthly sum such that one of the parents, usually the mother, can remove her/himself from the labour market and stay at home with their small children. In some circles this is construed as a threat to the building up and expansion of the day-care/kindergarten system and an undermining of women's right to work. This is of course part of an international trend. See Dorothy Smith's analysis of this situation faced by women in Canada and elsewhere, in her article 'The Underside of Schooling: Restructuring, Privatization and Women's Unpaid Work' (1998). Smith shows how '[i]deologies increasingly dominant in public text-mediated discourse in English-speaking North America wish to return women to traditional family values and traditional family roles'.

55 The problems arising from this issue were on the agenda in Norway back in the 1970s. Professor Erik Grønseth, the pioneer sociologist in this field, led the project entitled 'Men, too, as Part-Time Participants in Working Life' (see also Grønseth 1975).

sector. In Norway, this transition has been strongly marked by an expansion of the welfare state, with an increased demand for employment in the caring professions[56]. This expansion has been underwritten by a strong oil economy. Women's integration in the labour market has been supported by growth in the public sector. This growth has also been used consciously as a counter-cyclical policy. The right to work is enshrined in the Norwegian constitution and the number of unemployed is always a hot political question. Public employment in the service sector is used to keep unemployment numbers down (see Ellingsæter 1995b).

To sum up: Changes in the manual labour market have led to new challenges for the vocational fields in the secondary school programmes, which host 50 per cent of the youth between the ages of sixteen and nineteen. Vocational schools have shifted focus from training associated in general with the factory and home economics subjects to training for the changing industrial technologies related to an oil economy and the expanding social and welfare sector. Vocational education is central to the new reforms (*Reform 94*) in curriculum policy changes within the upper secondary school system. Vocational study programmes, in their particular ways, have been preparing the pupils directly for both family and working life. What I want to stress above all here are the internal constancies and changes in the vocational education sector, particularly with respect to gender.

56 We may ask what has happened to the redundant labour power during the past decades. Many of the skilled, semiskilled, and unskilled manual workers have ended up on disability pension, while their wives have gotten jobs in the service sector.

## Gender Traditions in Vocational Programmes

In the course of developing vocational training in the secondary schools following the Second World War, we have found the traditional division of labour by gender, which corresponds to the gender role patterns of the manual labour market and features the traditional view of women in the family sphere. The social organisation of masculinity and femininity has its particular form and is especially conspicuous in the vocational training programmes. It stands out as part of 'the natural order', to use an expression from Antonio Gramsci. The boys are to be found populating the 'hard fields' such as the mechanical, electrical, and the building trades in which they have been able to obtain apprenticeship contracts, craft certificates, and well paid, skilled jobs.[57] Some trades in the vocational programmes have had a mixed recruitment, such as hairdressers, cooks, waiters/waitresses, tailors, photographers, and dental technicians. Some of these programmes have also included courses that led to the completion of full training at school. Most girls, however, enter fields that have long been traditional for women. Often they are shorter courses such as home economics, health and social services, and the aesthetic subjects (Mjelde 1984a&c). These programmes have not led to apprenticeship contracts or craft certificates. Rather, they have been geared to the family sphere and lower-paid jobs in the service sector.[58] We find the same pattern, with certain variations,

57 Here I am referring to *possibilities* for complete training in a specific trade. If we take a closer look at the situation we find that many who have begun vocational training programmes over the past quarter century have never had the opportunity of completing their training to the level of the craft/trade certificate. One reason for this is that apprenticeship places are dependent upon the cyclical fluctuations in the economy, and competition for apprenticeships has been great as a consequence.

58 Gerd Stray Vogt, in her major work on the question of women in society, *Kvinnen i arbeidslivet. Kvinnen i dag* (*Women in Working Life: Today's Woman*), has made the following interesting point: '[I]n the sphere of the professions it is evident that full equality between the two sexes only applies within academic positions' (1950). However during the 1950s, admission to the

persisting in the expanded and developed vocational education sector in other Nordic countries (Grønbeck-Hansen 1993; Kaarninen 1994; Aarebrot 1991).

The expansion of the programmes of study in the school-based vocational sector and the apprenticeship scheme shot ahead quickly after the Second World War. Norway also ratified an apprenticeship law in 1950 directed toward the crafts and industrial sector, and particularly for men. The ideal of the nuclear family was in its historical ascendancy between 1945 and 1965. This was a period when the middle-class ideals, with father-as-breadwinner, were also being both upheld and realized in working class families. This was reflected in the expansion of the vocational training sector. Vocational schools for crafts and industry were expanded for boys and home economic programmes for girls. In the 1970s, changes began to be discernable in these traditions (Aamodt&Brandt 1982; Mjelde 1984b). The most sought-after male work in the manual labour market had shifted over to the expanding petroleum sector, leaving in its wake a shortage of labour power in the traditional male trades in the industrial sector. The journal *Bygningsarbeideren* (*The Construction Worker*) called for the recruitment of women into the building trades during the mid-1970s (Mjelde 1975c). The media began to dedicate time and space to women who were entering the traditional male world as welders and crane operators. At the same time, the women's movement had come strongly to the fore. Women's rights to education and wage work were advanced as issues essential to the liberation of women. Girls began to look for positions in the traditionally male fields of study in vocational education.

By comparing the number of girls in traditionally male fields in the year 1970–71 with the number in 1980–81, we find that there was an increase. Goldsmith in the latter decade was dominated by women. The proportion of girls rose from 30 per cent in 1970–71 to 80 per cent in 1980–81. In the field of the dental technician, 63 per cent were women by 1980–81; in the optical trades, 46 per cent; and in watchmaking, 37 per cent. Furthermore, these were all in subjects that were

---

academic professions was constricted by a prevailing ideology about women's place being in the home, although this is not a major point under discussion here.

taught completely in school. Here they avoided the scepticism which, in the labour market itself, greeted the very idea of girls becoming apprentices (see also Christiansen 1998). However, there was still scepticism among a number of the vocational teachers. In addition, there was an enormous competition for places in the training courses for these trades. True to tradition, many teachers did not 'see the sense' of accepting women. As one goldsmith teacher stated, 'They don't go on in the trade. They just get married and leave'.

Opposition to girls in these vocational fields took different forms in different trades. Other arguments were used in relation to trades that had a combination of vocational school and apprenticeship in their required course of studies. The main problem was to convince businesses to take in girls as apprentices. For example, in the graphics branch it was argued that the trade (typesetting) was too tough for girls – this in spite of the fact that technological developments had changed the tools, equipment, and work processes fundamentally. The argument in the building trades was that women in construction were often wedded to unattainable levels of on-the-job hygiene facilities.

This opposition has taken similar forms in all the Western industrial countries and has been well-documented by, among others, Paul Willis in *Learning to Labour: How Working Class Kids Get Working Class Jobs* (1977). It has been argued that to be tough and hard, to put up with heavy work for long periods, and to be able to lift heavy weights are essential to some jobs, and therefore are directly related to male body strength. Being skilled with mechanical equipment has also been part of the masculine value system. This protection of masculinity through biological argument has been one of the motivations for the strong opposition to women entering the skilled manual labour market. Such opposition has arisen from both the workers and their trade unions, as well as from those responsible for their apprenticeships, including employers.[59]

59 But this opposition has also tended to swing with the political and economic cycles. During World War II, as older readers in various countries will recall, the heavy industry factories were 'manned' mostly by women, since many men were away fighting the war.

Despite opposition, there was an upswing in the number of women working in the building trades in the 1970s. In 1980, ninety-nine women took the exam as machine operators and mechanics, and seventeen took the auto mechanics' examination. The greatest increase of women in those skilled trades that earlier had been filled by men was, however, in the graphics sector. In 1970, 2 per cent of the trainees were women; this had increased to 33 per cent by 1980. This increase has continued, and today 50 per cent of the graphics apprentices are girls (Mjelde 1984c, 1992).

In the 1980s, the integration of women into male-dominated spheres became a public question of educational policy. In Norway, as in the rest of the Nordic countries, a series of projects directed at the function of schooling were planned and implemented. These projects aimed to help women break the traditional gender division patterns in the manual labour sector (Christiansen 1998, 3–4). The organization 'Women in Men's Work (KIM)' was founded in 1978 by veterans of the 1970s female incursion into the crafts and industry sector jobs. Its members now became job counsellors in the schools, advising girls in their choice of vocation. A common Nordic project, 'Bryt-prosjektet' (Break the Barrier) worked to facilitate the breaking up of the traditional pattern of gender divisions in the manual labour market. The project came to an end in 1989 with the conclusion that, for that point in time, women in 'men's work' were experiencing a high rate of unemployment and many had ended their incursions into those fields.

## Reform 94 and the Move in the Opposite Direction

Gender-segregation in vocational training programmes was also the object of public attention in relation to the process that gave vocational training its renaissance. The demand for a level playing field in apportioning apprenticeship places between male and female applicants stemmed from the general goal of equal right to education.

This gradually won support both in the central political organs and in the Council for Vocational Training in Working Life (Høst 1997a&b).

On-going research in relation to *Reform 94* has taken up the question of the gender patterns of choice of occupation among young people.[60] Some of this post-*Reform 94* research is found in Michelsen, Høst&Gitlesen (1998) and in Sandberg&Vibe (1995). The Norwegian Institute for Studies of Research and Education (NIFU) made the evaluation in its report that gender segregation had been maintained or even strengthened through *Reform 94*. The point of departure was that when one focused on the number of sixteen-year-old girls who applied for positions in the foundation courses within the five traditionally male vocational areas – construction, the technical building trades, the mechanical line, the electrical line, and carpentry and woodworking – one found that the number of applications had sunk from 450 in 1991 to 221 in 1994. But further developments show that once again a higher number of sixteen-year-old girls applied for positions in traditionally male occupations. In 1996 their number was 357, and in 1997 the number had risen to 402. The numbers were approaching what they had been before *Reform 94*. Michelsen et al. have examined the development of the female portion of the cohort in the 1980s and 1990s. These young women began to study in the vocational training programmes and/or were learning in traditionally male-dominated fields, and they have found that the proportion that is composed of girls is small and stable. They found that only in two trades, joiner-carpentry and house-painting, were there increases in the number of girls. Within fields like plumbing, general carpentry, and the automotive trades girls make up only 1 or 2 per cent, and in the metal trades, 3 to 4 per cent. In the electrical trades there was a clear decline in the number of girls during the 1990s, something that can also be

60 The Ministry of Church, Education and Research in Norway has commissioned various research bodies to evaluate *Reform 94*. As a result of this initiative, various social milieus have had the chance to take up the task of making a contribution to establishing the research fundamentals considered necessary for professional evaluation of these reforms. This is the first time that research bodies in Norway have ever devoted attention to the interests of the vocational sector. Unfortunately these times seem to be over. It is nearly no research into the complexities of Vocational Education for the time being.

related to the restructuring of this branch in general in the late 1980s and the problem of obtaining 'a complete education' in the field (Berg and Lauritsen 1999).

The most important thing to happen with *Reform 94* was the achievement of a more equitable division in the vocational training system, and moreover, the establishment of a new branch of the economy within the traditional female sectors, namely, the caring professions and the professionalization of work with children and youth. These vocations have stemmed from home economics and caring as they were taught in the old vocational school. The basic health and social services training programmes, with their home economics and nurses' aid traditions, have been almost exclusively female-dominated. However, what is interesting here is that these sectors have seen an increase in the number of boys participating since *Reform 94*. In relation to the two largest trades within the health and welfare sector, 6.5 per cent of the training positions were occupied by boys in 1996, and 7.7 per cent in 1997.

In the 1990s, a public awareness about gender divisions in the labour market came to the fore, and it developed not only around the issue of getting girls into untraditional occupational choices, but also around getting boys to choose the caring sector. The project was called 'Conscious Educational Choices'. The Ministry of Church, Education and Research has consequently initiated its commitment to: 'strengthen vocational and educational counselling such that youth are better equipped to undertake *conscious educational choices* in relation to their own individual desires and needs, to the highest possible degree independent of traditional gender roles' (Christiansen 1998,).

The educational choices of youth can be paradoxical, and change and development in the vocational trades sector is complex. However, today one of the paradoxes is found in the fact that the boys seem to seek education which will equip them for shrinking sectors of the industrial labour market, while the girls are seeking education that allows them to take advantage of an expanding labour market in the field of the caring professions. The shrinking demand for skilled industrial labour power, which has continued to be the realm of working-class men, has not been very much studied in relation to gender (Nilsen 1996; Sande 1995). The endless changes in the labour market and in the family sphere, the great swings back and forth in terms of vocational form and content, and different signals from the public or official sphere – from the destruction of apprenticeship to the expansion of new fields – make it difficult to keep up with the changes. The only constant is change.

## The Expansion of Statutory Apprenticeships in Fields New to Women

After more than two decades (1976–1994) of a public policy debate and messages about the dismantling of the *Apprenticeship Act of 1950*, the *Apprenticeship Act 1980 (revised)* is now central to the current educational reforms. It has found its renaissance in both traditional crafts and industry trades and has been expanded to include new trades, especially in the automotive sector (Mjelde 1993).

The expansion of the caring sector in the labour market has required the expansion and coordination of new professional training in the vocational school system for the caring sector. This has meant great changes in girls' vocational education in recent years (Kløve 1993; Leithe 1997). Høst points out that the care workers' educational development toward specialized study programmes, apprenticeships, and craft-certificates started with initiatives during the 1980s in the fields of general education, as well as in the sphere of women's political demands. The demand at that time was to have completely equal rights to education in vocational trades; in other words, skilled work and professions for both genders (Høst 1997a&b). With *Reform 94*, new fields have been developed all the way to the level of craft certificates within occupations that traditionally in vocational education had been filled by girls, and which to that point in time had not had an entire programme of studies leading to a publicly recognized competence. In the 1980s, the Gender Equality Council of Norway defined these fields as areas which remained problematic pockets of education because they provided neither certificates of proficiency nor the requirements or competences for higher studies. What is novel in *Reform 94* is the development of new educational courses of study within the fields of care-giving, social work, and child welfare. This education leads to craft certificates in two fields care giving and child welfare. The programme is a combination of learning in school and learning that has an on-the-job aspect to it. The first two years consist of instruction in school and the remainder of the training, all the way to the craft certificate, is by apprenticeship.

Today's new jobs and skilled trades have their vocational educational roots in the old traditions of home economics, childcare, and training designed for nursing assistants. Teachers with a nursing or home economics background teach the training courses in these new fields. Both these types of teachers generally have their background in the care-giving field, but they tend to represent different traditions, and often look at things quite differently. Home economics teachers have had their education at the Stabekk College (now incorporated into Akershus University College) where their learning arena has been the kitchen (see Chapter 6). Nurses have had their training either through master-apprentice traditions in hospitals or at colleges. The home economics tradition has been directed toward family life. The nursing vocation has been directed toward the public nursing and care sector. The meeting between these traditions can often be pregnant with conflict.

Nurses have acquired their teaching experiences from the caring portion of the health and social welfare occupational training for nurses, and nurses' assistants from the vocational courses of study. This education has been anchored partly in working life by including half a year of guided practice in an institution as part of the course of studies. In the field of childcare training, where practical learning was a central part of instruction, the student had the chance to gain insight, and to experience vocational theory in practice, by working in an actual institution two days every week throughout the school year (Leithe 1995).[61] Leithe stresses that, in the current deepening and

61 This, moreover, is a pattern we also find in other occupational training in the vocational sector. However, there does seem to be a great variation in the different fields of the crafts and industry sector.

concretization of these training programmes in the school system, it remains important for the students to attain some of the practical experience of actual working life. In other words, in such situations, vocational theory can be directly related to the students' everyday life on the job in the institutions for which they are being trained, thereby making the theoretical work more meaningful. Vocational theory becomes integrated with what happens in the student's everyday life in the institution. The theory acquires meaning and significance for the students. The practice dimensions of these forms of education give possibilities for building up a form of teaching and learning in which practice and theory make up a whole. Both the fields of home economics in vocational education and nursing training have traditions of integrating theory with practice, especially home economics.

Home economics programmes (called 'lines' in the vocational schools) have, as well, been half-year or year-long courses and have been directed towards the family sphere. They have also functioned as preparatory courses for further education in the care-giving sector. The expansion of home economics teaching in the secondary schools' curriculum has at times been an integrated part of the vocational schools for crafts and industry (Nossum 1977). As mentioned above, the form and content of home economics teaching have reflected social views of women's role in society at different points in time (Mjelde 1999).

Norway's home economics college at Stabekk had a strong tradition of viewing men and women as belonging to distinct spheres of work. Stabekk had traditionally considered its mandate to qualify women to attend to the tasks of their gender's sphere of activity, and to do so in the best way possible. The closing words of the school's statement on the occasion of its fiftieth anniversary illustrate this very well: '[T]he school must always continue to see its task as working for the home life of Norway, of responding to the call that is symbolized by the flaming torch of knowledge on the school's banner: So clear a light for the country's fortune fair/Do women give knowledge of the home's warm care' (Anfelt 1989). Anfelt goes on to comment that the function of the school today (she wrote about the situation in the 1980s) is no longer in step with society's notion of the official ideology of the gender role division Nevertheless, developments at

Stabekk continued to be marked by the realities of society, wherein women and men remained each in her or his own sphere – a phenomenon that is also easily observed in the current developments in vocational curricula in the upper secondary school system. Be this as it may, with the changes in the labour market and the demands for gender equality both within and beyond *Reform 94*, new challenges to traditional gender patterns have been placed on the agenda.

## Conclusion

What, then, are the general tendencies in relation to the division of labour and gender in current developments in Scandinavia? In general, Birte Siim (1993) maintains that the answer is a series of contradictory tendencies within the Nordic welfare states. She argues that we might be on the way towards a woman-friendly state within parts of the public sector, while in other sectors we are moving towards a woman-neutral state, as for example in the field of higher education. Beyond this, in other sectors the traditional gender power relations are being reproduced, and with this, the gender-divided labour market.

Changes in technology, de-industrialization, the oil-economy, and the demands of women's right to obtain paid work – these changes have altered the traditional organization of knowledge as it has been manifested in vocational education. Women have, though to a lesser degree, entered traditional male spheres on the manual labour market. Women's right to a full skilled worker's certificate in the caring sector is changing the form and content of traditional female vocational training in secondary schooling. Craft certificates might also strengthen women's bargaining position on the manual labour market. But on the other hand, divisions still exist between the academic sector of upper secondary education, which gives the right to enter higher education, and the vocational sector, which prepares future workers for the manual labour market, as well as for office work and the caring professions. The interplay of gender and class in socialization processes of education and working life have been little studied in women's research in recent decades. It now seems these complex perspectives are coming more to the fore once again in women's studies and gender research (Ellingsæter et al. 1997, Nilsen 1996, Ve 1977, 1983).

CHAPTER 8

# Women and Apprenticeship: Industrial, Technological, Skills- and Gender-Related Changes in the Printing Industry in Norway

About twenty-five years ago, a rich debate broke out over the questions of women's participation in the manual labour market and their subordinate positions therein (Beechey, 1987, Cavendish 1982, Cockburn 1983, 1985, 1986, Glucksmann 1995). One of the characteristic features of female labour in the industrial sector has been that women have been concentrated in particular industries at particular levels where they have systematically been subjected to lower pay and poorer working conditions than their male workmates. The 'skills or competency question' also has its specific gendered history: more men than women have found their places in the skilled manual labour market, while most women have been in unskilled or semi-skilled jobs. In those trades marked by a division between skilled and semi-skilled labour, as in the printing trades, men have traditionally held the skilled positions. Traditionally in Norway, the field of bookbinding consisted of male bookbinders with four years of apprenticeship and female assistant bookbinders with two years of apprenticeship. The men who were bookbinders constituted more costly labour, while the women, with only two years of training, were cheaper. Consequently, the majority of workers on the bookbinding shop floor have been women. Bookbinders and bookbinder assistants received part of their training in the Norwegian vocational school system (Mjelde 1975c, 1984c, 1989, 2001).

The long-established division of labour on the manual labour market according to gender (and its concomitant vocational training) has been challenged in Scandinavia during recent decades. In the period between 1972 and 1992, the number of workers employed in industry in Norway fell dramatically, while the number employed in the social and personal services sector increased by over 350,000 (see Chapter 7, p. 142). The vocational schools, with their traditional gender segregation had to confront new challenges. The concept of competence with its four dimensions – learning competence, activity competence, production method competence, and social competence – has recently been introduced in the educational reforms in Norway. At the same time the traditional gendering of occupations has been challenged more and more. The official policy of the Norwegian state today is to get girls into traditional male trades and men into traditional female trades.[62]

Women have entered traditional skilled male trades for the past thirty years, but in almost insignificant numbers (Mjelde 2001, 242). Since the 1970s, the question of getting women into skilled trades has become an issue of high priority for both the women's movement and the state of many countries in the western industrialized world. As I explained in the previous chapter (see p. 147), women who entered the hard trades in Norway in the 1970s formed an organization, Women in Male Occupations (KIM) in 1979. They were carpenters, electricians, welders, auto mechanics, and engine drivers. But it seems that many of the women did not stay in the trades. Many went on to become teachers and counsellors.[63] There has been one exception: women have become a big part of the skilled labour force in certain sectors of the printing industry.

In my research project: 'Women and Apprenticeship: The Case of Printing' [1987], I visited twenty different workplaces in Oslo and Bergen in the late 1980s, and using a semi-structured questionnaire,

62 Another dimension is the policy of women's right to equal education and work side by side with men on the labour market and men's duties in relation to housework and childcare (Mjelde 2001, 243).

63 This might not be very surprising. There is huge variety between different trades. But many trades are physically demanding and are also tough male bastions with their special norms and values built up over the past hundred years. If one had the opportunity, this might be a tempting theme for further investigation. Another question is: have women in Norway entered trades where new skills are demanded, personal skills and qualities which traditionally have been socially constructed as female and feminine, such as neatness and punctiliousness?

interviewed sixty female apprentices and twelve male apprentices. I interviewed shop stewards and representatives of employers. I also asked the women to reply to certain questions in written essays. In addition, I looked into historical documents produced by the trade union organizations. I explored the following questions:

- What is the reason for such an increase of women in the printing trades in Norway in the past thirty years?
- Have the present technological changes resulted in specialization in the labour process that is less craft-oriented and perhaps closer to women's traditional labour roles?
- Are men leaving the printing trades?
- Have attitudes changed among the skilled men toward female labour power in the printing trades?
- Who are the women entering the trades?
- Why are they entering the printing trades?
- What is their outlook on the future?
- Do they see themselves as future workers or as future mothers?
- How do they perceive the possibility of combining work life and family life?

Some of the workplaces were old traditional printing houses with many employees; some firms however were newer, smaller industries and newspapers. Eleven of the women were apprentices in the newspaper business, forty-nine were in the printing industry, forty-five were compositor apprentices, ten were in lithography copying, three were in repro-technique, and two trained as printing press operators. It is apparent that women entered the pre-printing sector for the most part when they began to migrate to the printing industry in the 1980s. This is a tendency which has continued (Høst and Skarpenes 2000).[64] Forty-eight and one-third per cent of the women in the project were in their third year of apprenticeship, 26.7 per cent were in their second,

64 Mayer and Schutte (1984) shows that the same development occurred in Germany during the 1980s.

and 23.3 per cent were in their first year. The next section reports on some of my findings.

## The Background of the Apprentices and Their Vocational Training

Thirty years ago the typical recruit to the printing industry was the fifteen year-old lad who often had a family background in that same industry. He would come from compulsory grammar school and enter a half-year course in the vocational school before starting with an apprenticeship contract in a factory. He would enter the half-year course in the compositor class, the printer class, the lithographer class, the repro-photo class, the offset printer class, or the bookbinder class. He had twenty-five hours a week in the workshop and fifteen hours in the traditional classroom. In the traditional classroom he took Norwegian, arithmetic, social science, physical education, and theory connected to his trade, such as craft theory and technical drawing. Workshop activities and occupation-related theory were taught by vocational teachers, and the other subjects by academically trained teachers. He learned his actual trade in the school workshop. After six months he entered a three-and-a-half-year apprenticeship. He returned to school during these years for periodic training and finally to pass his qualification examination. Other youngsters started directly in a factory, and obtained their theoretical training at the apprenticeship school during certain periods of the training programme. This was regulated by the *Apprenticeship Act of 1950*.

In that same period, the training program for girls within the printing industry seemed to have been limited to classes that trained bookbinding assistants. The girls entered directly into an apprenticeship in a workplace and came to the vocational school for six weeks of practical and theoretical course work three times during their two-year apprenticeship. Their wages were lower than those paid to men, both during the time of apprenticeship and after qualification.

These patterns have changed during the last thirty years. The female bookbinding assistant classes no longer exist. Education for the printing industry has changed dramatically. In the period between 1970 and the 1990s, much more emphasis was placed upon training within the school system. The youngsters had two years of schooling in the school system before they started an apprenticeship. In the first year they passed through different stations, each representing the different sides of the production process within printing. In the second year they started in a special field and had a year of in-school training, for example, as compositors. Then they began a two-year period of apprenticeship.[65]

An investigation of technological change and its effects upon the labour force in general would shed considerable light on the gender contradictions involved with skills and labour in the printing industry. This would provide a solid context for seeing how these changes affect relations between men and women in this industry, specifically in regard to restructuring the labour processes and the consequences that this restructuring is having for the qualification of labour power. Another dimension is that the only thing that remains constant is movement, development, and change. D.J. Lee pointed out that the most serious weakness in the discussions around skills is a failure to conceptualize the ebb and flow of the manual labour market in depth. He also argued that the production processes are overlaid by the market process and that the labour contract is in practice being re-negotiated every second of the working day (1981). These processes are a feature of the experiential everyday life of the printing industry in 2001 as much as they were in 1981. The vice-president of the printers union said in an interview on August 7, 2001 that they were 'fighting the market situation every day and never knew what the next day would bring'.

Competition has been one of the significant and prevalent features of the manual labour market during the whole period of industriali-

65 With *Reform 94* the pattern of two years in school followed by two years of apprenticeship was instituted for all trades in Norway. But it is still possible to enter an apprenticeship contract directly with an employer.

zation.[66] Generally speaking, the dynamics of the labour market have never been static, and the element of competition has had an important function in lowering the labour costs. I refer to the general competition between old and young, men and women, and town and country and to the specific competition over the level of craftsmanship necessary for the different operations on the shop floor in the development of the modes of production (Beechey, 1987, Marx 1967). Here the issues around skills, competence, and qualifications have been important in the struggle between Labour and Capital. Earlier, the gender issue was systematically part of that struggle in general, and specifically in the printing industry. Men and women were put up against each other in the development processes in the printing industry and women were again and again on the losing side. When the linotype machine made its appearance in the nineteenth century, a struggle broke out over who was going to have the right to operate the new machines – men or women? Three women historians have described these struggles in different countries: Ingrid Andersgård shows that this struggle went on for thirty years in Norway, ending up with the men winning the right to operate linotype machines (1983). Ava Baron shows that the same contradictions and struggles took place in the USA in the same period, with the same results (1983). Brigitte Robak describes the same situation as it developed in Germany (1992). It should be noted that it has been women historians who have developed this new and interesting research. The new development in Norway however has been that women recently have taken over the skilled labour positions. In 1972, 2 per cent of the students entering the graphics classes in vocational schools were girls; in 1979–80, they made up 33 per cent; in 1986–87, 80 per cent. In 1996, half the apprentices who got their craft certificate were women.

Thirty years ago, one could well ask how many skilled positions in the average printing shop were inherited from father to son. The daughters were not invited into their fathers' male domain. Today it

66 Today the most prominent aspect of competition is so-called globalization, in which whole industries are moving around the globe to find cheap labour in their search of the maximization of profits. This affects vocational education, skills, and relations between men and women, but this is not at the centre of my arguments in this chapter.

might be different. Sixty-five per cent of the women in the project 'Women and Apprenticeship' had a working-class background. Twenty-five per cent of the fathers were part of the skilled working class. Twenty-five per cent had fathers in the printing industry. When asked who had influenced their decisions to enter the printing industry, 36 per cent said it was their mother and father, 6 per cent were advised by their mothers, and 30 per cent by their fathers. Eight-five per cent of the mothers were working outside the home; 25 per cent of these were skilled workers, while 65 per cent were in the unskilled labour force, such as home helpers, shop assistants, and factory workers. Lindgren, in his interesting discussion on changes in educational choice and social background in Sweden, points out that modern working-class daughters show androgynous or individual identification in their behaviour, unrelated to gender. He discusses, however, how daughters of 'career families' view their fathers as supporting and encouraging their choice of occupation within the traditional male sphere (2001, 270). One can ask whether this also has happened in printing families.

Competition has been strong for the available places in the printing classes in the vocational field of upper secondary schooling in Norway. In the 1986 school year, there were 550 applicants for the 110 available places in the first year of printing in the vocational school in Oslo. Eighty per cent of those accepted were girls. The girls were better qualified and were older than their male counterparts. Formal schooling, school marks, and age counted in the competition. The women in the project were highly qualified before entering the printing trade. Seventy per cent of the women in the project had their baccalaureate degree, that is, three years of general education after the compulsory school (graduation from grammar school/academic high school). Twenty per cent had finished other education, such as training as teachers and kindergarten teachers, child welfare workers, and hairdressers. The vice president of the printers' union indicated in an interview in 2001 that these trends of more highly qualified women have continued and led to women taking leading positions in the printing sector.

The building up of vocational education within the public school system has opened new opportunities to girls. Thirty years ago, when it was usual to go from grammar school into apprenticeships in a factory, the employers had full control of the intake to the trades. In the graphics branch it was argued that the trades were too tough for girls, and this argument was advanced long after technological developments had changed the tools, equipment, and work processes fundamentally. One can ask whether the traditional difficulties in obtaining apprenticeship contracts in male-dominated trades have been lessened. Is there something in the generic skills of girls that has contributed to the expansion of production, and simultaneously opened up recruitment of women into traditionally male skilled trades?

## Gender and Skills on the Factory Floor

One shop steward said:

> The girls are different from the boys. They are concerned about the craft and their own development, while the boys mainly learned to operate a machine and seemed content doing the same thing over and over again. The girls are different; they see more possibilities in the craft than the boys – lay-out, design, and the creative sides which are part of women. Those who have been trained in the vocational school before entering apprenticeship here have been very productive. Their attitude towards the craft is rather different from the boys'. The girls are more curious and want to learn more. It has two sides: the girls might not continue in industrial production, but anyway, they have been very productive while working here. It is impressive how much they know after two years of schooling. The factory has been an old fashioned institution, opposed to change. The boys who started as apprentices earlier entered the old patterns and did not object to anything, while the girls are more independent. They do not accept the way things are because there has been no change during the past thirteen years.

This quotation raises a lot of questions. Has there been a big difference in the disciplining of boys and girls in the working class? Is it the difference in age and the fact that the girls have a comparatively high general educational level before entering apprenticeship that makes them more independent and demanding? Are women simply more flexible than men? Are there qualities within the new labour processes that qualify women more than men for the new types of jobs? And how do the girls – and the male workers – experience these complex changes?

The relationship between gender and skills has brought about a rich debate in the academic world during recent decades. Braverman's analysis of the question of deskilling on the manual labour market, and his contribution to understanding women's work by highlighting the artificiality of skills categories are both insightful and problematic (1974). Braverman described fundamental traits in the development of the division of labour in industrialization, such as the division between intellectual and manual labour and the disqualification of work (see also Browne 1981, Sohn-Rethell 1978, Mjelde 1993). Braverman shows how skills on the manual labour market are socially constructed. One of his most important contributions to the discussion of women's work is, indirectly, his views about the artificiality of skills categories (Sanger 1989). Feminists took Braverman's idea further by exploring the extent to which divisions of male and female workers are artificial and have been shaped in the struggle between Labour and Capital over skills (Phillips&Taylor 1986).[67]

Phillips and Taylor maintained that the struggle between craft workers and employers centred on definitions of skills. Male workers organized politically to maintain their craft status by defining their jobs as more skilled than those of women workers. This process, occurring as it does in defiance of the declining technical complexity of their work, has led to a 'sexualisation of skill labels':

> [To] the extent that capital has succeeded in demolishing the actual craft knowledge and abilities of men workers, it has eroded the material basis for skill dis-

67 H. Braverman's *Labour and Monopoly Capital. The Degradation of Work in the Twentieth Century* taught me the complexity and contradictions in the development of vocational education on a higher level. His insights are very important in relation to understanding the division between mental/manual labour and vocational subjects versus academic subjects. I am aware of the criticism that labour process analysis ignores the valorisation side of the equation, including the question of time, which is an essential concern of economies. But I think his analysis is important for our understanding of fundamental aspects of vocational education, the subject of this book.

> tinctions, thereby creating a workforce with a thin layer of skilled men at the top and a mass of unskilled workers at the bottom. Men workers have fought long and hard against this process, fought to retain their craft position, and failing all else, at least their craft labels. And in these struggles, craft has been increasingly identified with masculinity, with the claims of the breadwinner, with the degree of union strength. Skill has been increasingly defined *against* women – skilled work is work that women don't do] (Phillips&Taylor 1986, 63).

Phillips and Taylor point to the importance of examining the labour process, as well as the structure of labour markets, in order to understand both the sexual division of labour and gendering of labour skills. Moreover, the authors take account of the active role workers play in shaping the labour process through their struggles and collusion with employers. In doing so, Phillips and Taylor highlight the ways in which the skills definitions of jobs come to stand for things other than the content of those jobs; in other words, skills definitions are an aspect of social relations, including gender relations, and cannot be regarded as straightforward indices of job content.

In her study of printers, Cynthia Cockburn (1986, 1985, 1983) has criticized Phillips and Taylor for portraying skills definitions as entirely ideological: '[U]nless we recognize what measure of reality lies behind the male customary over-estimate of his skill we have no way of evaluating the impact of electronic photocomposition, the leeching out of the tangible factors of skill from some tasks and their relocation in others, out of the compositors reach' (Cockburn 1986, 105).

Veronica Beechey has noted the inadequacy of interpretations that assert, as Phillips and Taylor do, a universal tendency of capitalist development to de-skill workers and their jobs (1987). It is important to specify different dimensions of skill, and to recognize the ways in which capitalist production continually generates new skill requirements while destroying other skills.

Another point of view of gender dynamics and the development of skills in labour process analysis is that the feminization of jobs is synonymous with de-skilling. Ava Baron (1987) points out in her article, 'Contested Terrain Revisited: Technology and Gender Definitions of Work in the Printing Industry, 1850–1920' that the idea that women embody de-skilling, that they are tools used by capital to de-skill labour, remains unchallenged. The development of the printing industry in Norway over the past decades of technological transformation challenges this notion. Women have entered the skilled manual labour market in the printing industry, and they have taken over well-paid jobs.[68] The training for the jobs has also been developed and is on a higher level today than it was twenty years ago.

Braverman is criticized for the static aspect of his analysis. It is argued that he has not taken into consideration the ongoing, living struggle between Labour and Capital on the manual labour market. The struggle around vocational training has played a multi-facetted role. Today, the level of skill of the labour force in the manual labour market in Norway is higher than ever before. The unions have been active in these achievements (see also Høst 1997a&b [b]). When it comes to job content and control over educational and labour processes in times of restructuring and upheaval, the struggles of trade unionists have played an important part (Lesjö 1979).

If one were to take Braverman's argument to the utmost consequence when it comes to the thesis on de-skilling, vocational training and apprenticeship would not exist.[69] The thesis of de-qualification has created a rich debate, and empirical research has complicated the understanding of these processes. Braverman has made an important contribution to our understanding of the development of Taylorism in the manual labour market and the need for capital to control labour power. He describes general trends in the development of production under industrial capitalism, but inside this framework there has been considerable scope for organizing

68 The interviews were conducted in a period of economic prosperity in the printing industry of Norway. The industry was expanding and the need for skilled labour power was high. Norway went into a recession in 1988, a factor that might have affected my informants, but not my main arguments in this chapter. However, it would be interesting to interview them a second time to see how market fluctuations affect their experiences and perceptions.

69 Braverman's main frame of reference is North America. Vocational training and apprenticeship in North America and Europe might generally have undergone very different and divergent developments. North America has imported a lot of its skilled labour from Europe (Maurice&Sellier 1979, Wolf 1982). It is to the point that Canada's name for one of its ministries is the Ministry of Employment and Immigration.

production in different ways. The American tradition has been to eliminate from the shop floor as much brain work as possible. The European tradition has been to keep more skilled labour on the factory floor (Castro&Carvalho 1985, Mjelde 1986, Wolf 1982).

The question of skills has also proven to be an important productivity factor, and vocational training has been built up parallel to the development of the industrialization process. There is a generic need, in any society based on advanced manufacturing, for a technically knowledgeable labour force. Any hierarchically organized form of advanced manufacture, capitalist or socialist, needs both a general labour force with the basic cognitive skills to follow abstract rules and perform operational details, and other workers with a sufficient level of specific knowledge in specialized fields to coordinate and design production systems (Livingstone 1987, Mjelde 1987).

What is distinctive about advanced capitalism's educational needs is that they are continually changing. They change as the central production techniques are revolutionized in competitive pursuit of profits. The question of gender is not of central importance. Rather, the question is how to extract the most profit out of the labour power (see also Roldan 2001). The vice-president of the printers' union expressed this in the following way: 'Today it is the old skilled workers who have had difficulties in the transformation process. They are the ones who have to leave when it is a question of layoffs. It's not the skilled women who have to leave. They do not get laid off' (2001).[70]

## Is Social Competence a New Productive Factor on the Shop Floor?

One of the questions I wanted to explore in my study was how the women who have entered the male-dominated terrain of the printing shop floor experienced gender contradictions. How did they

70 Personal interview 2001.

experience their womanhood, the recognition of their skills and knowledge in relation to the question of gender in their everyday lives? The girls were asked to give a written account of how they experienced their situation. The essay question was, 'Is it your experience that your male fellow workers accept you as part of the skilled labour force?'

Eighty per cent of the apprentices made positive statements about their experience with their male fellow workers, 19.5 per cent found that the relations were completely problem free, while 0.5 per cent reported negative experiences. Here are some of the responses:

> The boys' attitude toward more girls in the trade is generally positive, I think. If once in a while I feel unjustly treated, it is most often because of the contradiction between skilled workers and apprentices rather than those between men and women. (*Siri, 20 years old*)

> The boys are scared that we will become better than they are and might be better liked by the boss who is always a man. They tend to pay attention to your mistakes, making sure you are not too good. They often look at women as temporary labour power, until kids and home take us away. We are there to make the environment softer and more pleasurable for them. (*Kari, 28 years old*)

> As apprentices they received us well. They felt that they needed women in the work environment. But when four young women entered, they felt in the minority and were scared that the women would take over. The younger guys are more positive than the older ones, who are often sceptical and at times negative. The leaders are all men and they pick the women first for the lousy jobs. (*Berit, 25 years old*)

> I experience that my fellow workers do not care whether you are a man or a woman. It is the work leaders, who are all men, who care about that. And whether or not they want girls as leaders/bosses is a different matter. (*Bibbi, 34 years old*)

> I think the people I work with are really okay, but I don't have such a good relationship with the bosses (functionaries). There is too great a division between workers and functionaries, which often leads to trouble. (*Tone, 19 years old*)

The comments here explore much of the complexity in these women's experiences of everyday life on the factory floor. Siri emphasizes that the 'conflicts is between the men as skilled workers and the women as apprentices. There have been long traditions in the manual labour market where tradition has given the right to the elders 'to push around' the new apprentices. They have been given the dirty jobs and they have been running the errands, and the different trades have had 'initiation rites' (Mjelde 1990a). Kari emphasizes the competitive aspects of the relationship, and that the men look upon them as temporary labour power. Berit talks also about the competitive aspect with regard to the number of women. When the women became a majority in their work section, the men were afraid that 'the women are taking over'. She emphasizes also the question of age, saying that the younger male workers are more positive than the older. Berit, Bibbi, and Tone all agree that their fellow workers are all right but that the leaders and division of labour are problematic. Berit says that the leaders are all men and they pick the women for the lousy jobs.

The male shop steward in a big factory of eight hundred workers[71] made the following comments about contradictions between men and women:

> I don't think the contradictions lie in the relationship between men and women. The girls have managed to gain respect. They do men's work. The contradictions lie between old and young, between skilled and unskilled. The girls who come here feel more qualified than many of the men, and they let people know about it. Many of the skilled workers here are retrained, they have been working with lead for many years, and they don't feel secure. They often don't handle the job as well as the girls. Some work more slowly and need more explanations. And they are knocked out by these young girls! There are few hard contradictions between men and women, but they exist between young and old and around the issue of general knowledge – the girls have much more general knowledge.

The shop steward emphasizes here that the girls are more qualified, that they do a better job than the men. He says they have more general knowledge and that this makes them in general more productive. Are they more socially competent than their male comrades, who were often trained in the mechanical, hands-on, Tayloristic masculine, work of, for example, the lead type-setting process? We can ask whether an increasing level of general knowledge has become a new productive

71 Fifteen of the girls I interviewed worked at this factory.

factor on the shop floor and if so, why women in this production field appear to be more successful than men of similar age and class background?

The vice-president of the Norwegian Graphics Union made the following analysis:

> The print workers today have to take part in holistic labour processes, right from the design of the products to dealing with customers. You must be an employee who has a unified view of the product, all the way from the work of the hand to communication with the customer. You need social competence, the ability to communicate and discuss with customers. The old vocational education did not have any of those dimensions. The men were trained to execute labour-related operations, between them and the lead, between the machine and the man. Today the women seem to have more of the necessary abilities. They also seem to take over leadership positions in the industry. That was unheard of twenty years ago (2001).

The findings in my research projected support these observations. Few studies have actually gone into a detailed analysis of the needs of training in the different sectors of the manual labour market. Labour market theorists have largely ignored the need for an understanding of the vocational training and apprenticeship systems that train the workforce for the manual labour market. The educational level of the young girls in this study is high, both on the general level and through their training in the vocational school system. They have more education and training than ever before for the jobs performed. The project indicates that women are taking over the highly paid skilled jobs of men in the printing industry. Jane Jenson, in 'The Talents of Women, the Skills of Men: Flexible Specialization and Women', argues that the restructuring of the labour process so as to privilege skilled work and workers will further marginalize women. Following Cockburn, Jenson argues that women are excluded from developing a familiarity with technology. She goes on to argue that traditional women's abilities are viewed as 'natural' talents, rather than acquired skills. She suggests that women will lose out in a restructuring process that favours skilled work and workers (1988). Recent developments in the labour market in Scandinavia, such as in the printing trades, partly challenge these assumptions (Ellingsæter 1997, 2000, Mjelde 2001).

To develop further our understanding of the contradictions between men and women in the manual labour market, I propose that we analyze from a historical perspective the processes through which skills (qualifications) are developed, acknowledged, and compensated for both in the vocational school system and in the workplace. The experiences of these contradictions in people's everyday lives should be at the core of the research (Daly&Mjelde 2001, Jensen 1997, Smith 1987). Another dimension of the social construction of the complex relationship between men and women on the manual labour market is to look into new inequalities between women. Empirical work in the field shows similarities in various countries, but also variations. Rudolf Husemann, on the basis of my data, proposed looking at the gender question in relation to the hierarchical composition of the work place.[72] Such analysis is relevant and necessary to our understanding of the complex gender division of labour on the manual labour market (see also Cohen&Zysman 1987; Ellingsæter 1997; Ellingsæter& Rubery 1997; Ellingsæter 1999; Sande 1994).

72 I would like to thank the members of the European VET network for valuable comments and input. In addition I owe great gratitude to Martha Roldan of FLACSO, Buenos Aires, Argentina, who has kindly shared her time and given me her valuable comments on this issue.

Figure 9: Knowledge of the domestic sciences in the 1960s. The classes are no longer segregated for girls and boys.

# Part Three

# Workshop Learning, How Does It Really Work?

CHAPTER 9

# Bridging Praxis and Research: Vocational Teachers on the Journey from Work to Learning, from Learning to Work[73]

Vocational didactics, experience-based learning, responsibility for one's own learning and project-based learning are new concepts in both the vocational courses of study in secondary schooling and in the pedagogy of professions. A vast expansion of study programmes has occurred in college and university education over the last thirty years in Norway as elsewhere. The contradictions between different learning arenas in craft-related fields, like medical and architectural studies, have developed with the expansion of learning within the walls of formal education. However, one finds the same contradictions in all fields, not least in teacher education. One feature of this has been the toning down of demands for practicum experience in working life, either before or during the course of studies, as in the curricula of nursing and engineering. This development has created new problems; new challenges are rising across the whole spectrum of formal education. This has created new demands for change. In teaching this has led to a change in focus from the teacher being front and centre in the classroom – teaching and instructing – to the learner being at the centre with the teacher filling the role of facilitator or counsellor. Mentoring has become the new mantra in teacher education as an

73 This chapter is based on my own experience teaching vocational teachers how to research and write for their MA (Masters Thesis) in vocational pedagogy. They are trained themselves in a trade and they have what we call 'a double praxis'. They have received training in pedagogy from evening and weekend courses, most frequently while working as teachers in vocational schools. Together with my colleague Tove Lien, I conducted a research project into their experiences in the 1990s, which provided the empirical basis for this chapter (See Lien&Mjelde 1999).

element for enhancing reflective practice in teachers, as well as within the professional developments of schools as a whole (Sundli&Ongstad 2003).

Vocational teacher education has its special history in the development of teacher education in Norway and, to the present, the only place in Scandinavia that has a Masters programme in Vocational Pedagogy in the Akershus University College.[74] During its fifty years of existence, pedagogical education of vocational teachers has mainly been given as in-service training courses. The Masters programme has been functioning since 1975 and is organized as part time studies extending over four years. It has now produced scholarly and scientific knowledge from the complex world of vocational education for thirty years.

The pedagogical education for vocational school teachers arose as a political question with the expansion of vocational schooling in craft and industry after the Second World War. Pedagogical courses started for vocational school teachers in 1947. The first cohort was composed totally of men, mainly from the mechanical engineering sector. These teachers instructed in the industrial workshops during the day and the pedagogical courses were given as evening or weekend classes. This model has had the advantage of the students being in real work situations while studying, yet the curriculum for vocational teachers has not been without its conflicts.

One of the dilemmas in the development of vocational teacher education in higher education over the last fifty years is the question of how one can arrange for learning that is based on an experiential workers' culture. Anne-Lise Høstmark Tarrou (1997, 60) describes this dilemma as follows:

> It is possible to argue that college teachers of pedagogy in the vocational studies sector implicitly carry within them the scientific method of thinking promoted in the universities, and that these teachers apply this in their own way in order to teach vocational teachers, ignoring the accumulated knowledge of the vocational fields themselves. This can create an unintentional and untenable situation for the vocational students.

74 The University of Gothenburg, Sweden, has recently started a Masters programme in vocational pedagogy.

These dilemmas have been highly visible in the development of vocational teacher education and have been a challenge to academic teachers who mainly have a university background. But important empirical work has been done during the past decades, investigations into these dilemmas by Masters students of vocational pedagogy; these studies have shed new light on the field and its complexities (Strøm 1994, Austenaa 2005). The Masters students are encouraged to do their research in relation to their own praxis as vocational teachers. Their praxis and their everyday life in their workplaces are often central in the four years they work on their Masters thesis.[75]

## Vocational Teachers, Their Background and Specific Assumptions about Learning

What is characteristic of the background of vocational teachers is a practice-based world from a sector of working life that is outside the educational system. Most frequently they have had vocational training and practice in the manual labour market before they became teachers.[76] Among other vocations, the students in this programme are composed of skilled people such as electricians, auto mechanics, carpenters, cooks, nurses, and home economics teachers. There is a great variation of background and age among the Masters students.

75 I am here saying they are encouraged to take their own praxis as a point of departure for their thesis work. But they are of course free to choose any subject to work on. My experience over the past fifteen years indicates that most of the students want to understand and research problems they meet as vocational teachers in their everyday life. Their empirical work into the ongoing dilemmas in the upper secondary school system during the past decade has been an important source of inspiration for me.

76 One group of students we have in the Masters programme is composed of home economics teachers. They trained at the former National Home Economics Teachers College, now part of Akershus University College, in the Department of Vocational Teacher Training. What they have in common with the vocational teachers is that one of their learning arenas is their workshop: the kitchen.

Gender composition reflects the gender role patterns that have distinguished family ideology and the manual labour market in the various phases of industrialization. For the most part we find the male teachers in the 'hard' fields, and the women in the caring professions and the aesthetic subjects (see Chapter 6–8). They have gained their work experience from hospitals, building sites, handicraft and industrial firms. They themselves have often been vocational students and apprentices and, as such, have undergone workplace learning and journeyman/apprentice relations. They have mastered their specialty in 'learning by doing' relationships. They bring this learning experience with them into their work as teachers, and they practice workshop learning in the course of their teaching jobs.

The vocation itself and the carrying out of the vocational exercises are central to the relations of learning. Lennart Nilsson (1986) describes the vocational didactic involved here in detail, as the relation between the student and the task. The work activity itself is the rotation point for learning. The hospital or the restaurant kitchen and the automotive workshop also provide a social structure in which one can see the Masters, journeymen and apprentices at work. One learns in relation to others. One receives supervision and hands-on guidance from other apprentices, journeymen and Masters. One learns through observation and by emulating models, both socially and vocationally. The vocational school teacher brings these experiences with them into the formal school structure.

Another specific feature of vocational teaching is that the lessons are linked to changes and developments in on-going production life, where the only constant is change. For the teachers, then, the process of acquiring skills to teach in the vocational field is a constant process of 're-skilling' from work in the production and service sectors to the teaching field. In the course of acquiring their skills competence, vocational teachers are socialized into a fundamental grounded understanding and outlook, as their trades change in concert with political and economic changes in society; their vocational competence is, as well, related to their ability to cope with these changes.

Through their vocational competence and experience, vocational teachers are socialized with a very basic understanding that the vocations change in step with technological changes in society. Their vocational knowledge has, at the same time, an internalized sense of the subject's historical and production tradition with its norms and values that lead and regulate the learning process. In the handicraft trades one finds gradually accumulated knowledge that has been developed over a long period of time. This is characterized as constant, functional, effective, rational and enduring in the work process. Much of this knowledge is not articulated, and much of the work in the Masters programme has precisely to do with the student's own efforts to put into words the unsaid, and to find concepts for expressing this knowledge. The practically determined consciousness might be a compression of experience that has still not been put into words (Gamble 2004, Molander 1993, Tempte 1982).

One of the purposes of the Masters programme in vocational pedagogy is to put the experiences of vocational school teachers into words. Their double praxis background, their experiences of learning a trade and practicing their trade in working life, and their experience as vocational school teachers in upper secondary schools, are the core of the teaching and learning processes. An experience they have from their teaching situation in the upper secondary schools is the meeting with their academic colleagues who teach Norwegian, foreign languages, and the natural sciences. These teachers are mainly trained in colleges and universities and frequently they have no experiences from any other world but the educational institutions[77]. It is not necessary to possess a vivid imagination to understand that the meeting between these two worlds and two cultures can be challenging. The new reforms have put more and more demands on how to organise teaching and learning to make the twain meet. In this end, concepts and features highly visible in workshop learning are now central to the general education debate – like master-apprentice working and learning relations and situated learning. However, these

77 This is a general problem in the development of schooling and has been at the core of discussions also in general teacher education. The Tvind School in Denmark required that students entering the Teacher Training College first work one year in a factory or on a farm before being admitted. This problematic has of course been present in the development of teacher education in many places of the world.

terms are very often bandied about without any connection to the traditions that gave rise to them.

Behind this increasing interest in project-based work, problem-oriented teaching and experience-based learning lies the crisis in the school system and the increased recognition of the separation of the teaching from the participants' everyday reality and its frequently vast distance from working life (see Chapter 5). One attempt to overcome this separation is to make the teaching situation conform as much as possible to everyday life and experience. This is a technique that we find in practically-oriented forms of education to recreate links between life and learning. Henning Salling-Olesen (1985) writes that in all adult education there is a need for broad, fundamental insights into the student group's life and assumptions, the vocation and the vocation's possibilities, and the education system's framework and assumptions. A pedagogy that does not pose questions based on the experiences of both students and teachers stands in danger of instilling a conservative practice unsuited to a changing world. What is basic is investigation into, and reflection about the material reality that the students come from. It is very important to recognize this material in relation to how our identities are formed, and of course the praxis that springs from material conditions. The understanding of experience is, of course, also directed culturally by means of shared social values, language and narrative forms – all of which give form to the way we understand our lives. It also follows from this that learning is influenced by the emotional circumstances in which it takes place. Another feature of human relations is different points of view, opposing outlooks and values. Conflict and social antagonisms cannot be wished away but are factors constantly present in social relations (Foucault 1992).

Anne-Lise Høstmark Tarrou (1995, 101) describes the branch of studies for the field of crafts and industry as a conflict meeting point between two vocational cultures, that of experience-based working class culture, and the culture of academic general education. In his doctoral dissertation which deals with the development of programmes of vocational education in secondary schooling, Per Drevvatne (1983) has shown that the situation existing between the teaching groups in upper secondary education was marked by an almost total lack of communication between teachers with vocational or classroom backgrounds, especially with regard to pedagogical questions. Tor Halvorsen (1994, 118) maintains that the value and identity conflicts that we can observe between vocational teachers and general/theoretical teachers clearly shows that the pedagogical, social and cultural position of vocational teachers are in retreat.

This conflict-filled meeting point is also expressed through the division between different learning experiences at work and at school, and between workshop and classroom. This division reflects the division of labour and value system of society in general. This value system reveals an over-evaluation of academic education and intellectual work, and an under-evaluation of vocational education and manual labour (Bourdieu&Passeron 1977, Grignon 1971). The conflicts also involve the fact that experiences gained in the manual labour market and the education system represent different social and cultural relations where not only the methods of thinking, but also the jargon and terminology of working life and its social relations are very different. When it comes to learning, the problems and possibilities of working life for the academically trained are not the same as the problems and possibilities found in the vocational courses of study. Even where vocational learning at school is organized toward practical working life, it is still separated from actual working life both physically and through different organization, power dynamics and culture. Practical training at school has characteristic features that are different from those in the workplace. Knowledge is organized and dealt with in a school-specific manner (Berner 1989, 45).

The challenge for Masters students is how to put into order the processes they take from their own experiences of an experience-based worker culture, which is now being put under the spotlight, and the need to sharpen their analytical tools in order to understand and describe this reality. A general research problem requires an increase in understanding of the processes of change in the different trades, the conditions for change in vocational programmes of study, and what consequences these changes have for teacher education. How to formulate relevant research topics and make them operational and research worthy? One challenge for those of us who are the teachers is how to organize the studies such that the students' experiences of the contradictions are at the core of the study and how to organize the learning and teaching processes from 'praxis to theory.' This raises a number of questions. How to develop scientific thinking and train the students in researching and writing by using their own experiences and encourage students to support each other and work together in groups?

## Time and Place, a Learning Fellowship

One of the questions is what effects do the contradictions they experience in their everyday life and in the hegemonic order have on the relationship between research and teaching, counselling and learning in these students' vocational pedagogy projects? How much real significance do the students' actual experiences have in terms of the content and organization of the programme? What does it mean when we say that the students have different experiences that once again are the basis for learning processes in these programmes? Or to put it in another way, how does the student develop his or her own knowledge, moving out from his or her own practice? When we, who teach from an academic learning tradition, say 'It is through concepts that we grasp the world,' this becomes a major problem for many students. Jon Frode Blichfeldt (1992) describes a model where he distinguishes between practice-oriented and theory-oriented knowledge. This distinction divides reflected from non-reflected knowledge, and relational and non-relational knowledge. When one is aware of what one does, is capable of, and knows, one's knowledge is relational and reflected. When one learns by rote, without knowledge and awareness, the knowledge gained is not relational and not reflected.

One of the questions posed by those of us who teach the Masters students is how does knowledge become reflected and relational. Gry, who had many years of experience teaching dental technology in vocational studies, was working on a Masters thesis on the development dental-technician proficiency and competence learned, formerly as a craft vocation in the vocational schools and apprenticeships, to its current elevation as a university college programme. Erik and Ole wrote a thesis on the development of a comprehensive vocational training programme for the fields of Electro I and Electro II. During their monthly gatherings at the college, the students give each other advice and counselling on their individual projects. This often has to do with the relationship between the vocation as a whole and its actual *praxis*. What does the shift from craft work practice to an academic course of studies mean for the practical dimensions of that vocation? What are the similarities and differences between dental technology and the electrical fields in relation to the nature of theory and practice in the specific vocation? Large sections of the electrical field have been 'theoreticised'. Prospective vocational students now go to school for two years before they are allowed even come into the vicinity of a practical work situation. What consequences does this have for the students in relation to the practical dimensions of their chosen field, and how does it affect the relationship between theory and practice in the vocation itself?

The engagement of the students and their supervision of each others work, gradually lead to more nuanced and qualified discussions and fundamental analyses of similarities and differences between the historical knowledge that is at the foundation of the different vocations. The questions they pose are as follows. How are we to understand these differences? How are we going to obtain knowledge about these questions? Such questions lead to discussions about what the field of vocational pedagogy and development is all about. One of my new students, who had been sceptical about this approach, sent me an email admitting that after experiencing group work, she found that it brought new ways of seeing things into the light of day.

The approach to problems that are developed from such discussions in the Masters programme can be purely vocational and technical, for example, the development of new technology in the electrical field, new teaching materials and procedures in the needle trades. On the other hand the problems posed might be oriented to vocational didactics such as the organization of learning in general so as to gain increased activity and motivation in the foundation course for industrial design. Many students also study the effects of Reform 94, both in connection to schooling and to apprenticeships. Some students have mapped out the contents of the reforms in the health and caring professions and the electrical fields. They examine the effects of new organization of the first two years of study at school. What is happening with the integration of the vocational and general fields? How can one organize project-based teaching in one's own field or vocation? Others map out the transition from school to apprenticeship placement. Who gets the apprenticeships? How do they experience their learning situation during their apprenticeships? How does learning at school compare with learning at work? How is the guidance function undertaken in the work situation?

Other students map the effects of the reforms in adult education. The Masters students bring to light new knowledge from the field of vocational education. One student said that he got the feeling that it was the students themselves who actually brought vocational pedagogy into reality, and that the strength of the Masters programme lay in capturing the vocational experiences of the students.

## 'Learning by Doing' While Writing a Masters Thesis

The students begin the Masters programme working in groups on concrete writing projects. We as teachers stress the method of working in groups, and cooperation with each other is at the core of the curriculum in vocational pedagogy. Throughout their course of studies the students work with questions linked to their vocation and the learning processes and they are encouraged to cooperate. In the first stage of the programme, which extends for two years on a part-time basis, this is carried out by working on three mini-projects. This phase of the programme concludes with an examination project. The mini-projects provide training in developing theoretical perspectives based on one's own practice, and subsequently to develop fruitful topics and materials for research and development projects, to provide training in various methods of research and development work, as well as for evaluating the processes they and the others are undergoing.

The progression of the programme of studies builds on the work of verbal description of the students' own reflections about their experiences in such a way as to lead to more general and more collective comparisons and principles. There is a systematic coverage of experiences and discoveries, and this, with the help of auxiliary empirical research, makes the shift from the verbal to the written possible. A student in the third year said[78],

> The experiences I myself have had in connection to learning during vocational training are relevant to this programme because the activity itself is central. The activity is to produce something concrete – the project assignments. These activities have taken place in relation to advisors and students. The productions have happened through skilled counselling by a master and from input by other journeymen and apprentices. The journeymen are those who have come furthest in some areas than the other students. The apprentices have been students with less experience. But these roles have shifted, of course, from one theme to the next. In one situation you can be a journeyman, and in another, a master.

Many vocational teachers recognize this learning model either consciously or unconsciously from their own vocational training, where the progressive phases of learning are linked to the foreman/instructor explaining, the apprentice following, the instructor showing, the apprentice watching, the apprentice doing as instructed, the instructor correcting, the apprentice repeating, the instructor correcting again (Olsen 1992, 15).

The activity itself is the starting point both for instrumental and relational learning; this is the standard pedagogical model one finds in craft-oriented education. It is an ideal typical model and there is of course a great deal of variation in its practical application. There was not much awareness of these problems 30 years ago. Many have gone through the learning period in their apprenticeship without any organized guidance whatsoever. One Masters student who had trained as a nurse twenty-five years earlier described her study time as a master-apprentice relationship in which the master had neither time

78 Student citations included in this chapter have all been directed to me, as teacher and counsellor, by my Masters students, usually by email, or earlier in the form of written answers to a questionnaire given to Masters students in vocational pedagogy by Tove Lien and Liv Mjelde (Heikkinen, Lien&Mjelde 1999).

nor inclination, nor sufficient understanding to provide guidance to the apprentice nurse. The education bore the imprint of 'learning on the job', which implies developing the quality of one's practical skills without any particularly theoretical basis (Prestbakmo 1997, 2). By contrast, in our Masters programme in vocational pedagogy, it is the counselling relationship that provides the main dynamic. During their learning processes the students are asked to analyze their experience by reconstructing it. They must then reflect on this reconstructed experience and evaluate it. The articulation is a social process. The relationship between students and advisors is extremely important in this process. The advisor has a responsibility for leading the group processes as well as giving individual counselling on each project.

One of the students reported that she found it frustrating at first to have her own experiences pulled into the course of studies. She was not used to such a form of learning: 'So little lecturing, but group work and your own experiences. Only now when I know more do I see why it was done this way, and that this is a very practical way to learn. We have a tradition that we come to a study place where we will be lectured to.' This student came from the home economics tradition, a form of education that has had its vocational training within the year-long school curriculum.

The students come from all over the country to gatherings at the college six times a year. The explicit trajectory of the part-time organization of the Masters programme consists of a movement away from work, into study, and then back, from study to work again. On one hand, the students' everyday life is full of their own pupils' and colleagues' expectations, and demands from the everyday life at school, and on the other hand, the demands and expectations that are posed by scientific and scholarly thinking.

In the work process undertaken during these gatherings we place great stress on developing constructive, cooperative working relations between students such that they also work together in the intervals between gatherings. In addition to counselling one another in groups throughout the study programme, they use each other's work in the course of documenting their own thesis project. The groups are intended to function as a safe working forum and a secure environment for study such that everyone has the possibility to formulate and analyze the specific research issue which she or he has taken up, as well as those of their fellow students. Such a group forum involves a gathering and a concentration of resources, in terms of both counselling and teaching. For the most part the actual lecturing is related to the students' research themes within the group forum. The basis for discussion in the group is selected written material that has been produced by the students in the periods between gatherings, and which has been sent out to each of the group's members and advisors in advance of the gathering. On the basis of this written material, the students advise one another in the group. They work with one another's material by means of professional and vocational discussions and common counselling sessions. This counselling work strengthens reflection about one's own work and deepens relations within the groups. As one of the students put it, 'You get an amazing number of new insights from your fellow students.'

We stress the development of the study environment both because it is fundamental to the learning processes in the programme and because only a few have a working environment where they can work through problems associated with their Masters thesis work. One of the students said, 'A large part of the problem is even being allowed to have input and ideas, and to get them accepted at the workplace.' There is often very little access to vocational literature at the home location and few opportunities to talk about the literature. Furthermore, even taking up higher education can in itself create problems at the schools where the students work. Many colleagues at school view the Masters programme as 'academicisation' something that the participants use as a means for moving out of their social group in pursuit of social mobility. It is not uncommon for Masters students to say that their colleagues at school either show little or no interest in their Masters work, or they greet it with mistrust and negativity (Lien 1991).

One of the main problems in the programme of studies is related to the writing process itself and the students' own creation and development of written materials. The students begin to write from the beginning of the programme. The mini-projects are intended to get them writing, working with texts, and to learn scientific and scholarly methods of work. One student observed:

> I had to go through a process of using 'the pen'. The writing process was heavy going right from the first mini-project up to the exam project. But with every *project* the pen got easier to use. The theory took on new content. The thoughts became exciting and challenging and it was especially exciting to see how I expressed them in words. It was as though my thoughts and reflections took on a new dimension that made me better. I was more secure in what I knew and in my field.

The students' work goes through different phases in the course of the programme. In the first study period the work is marked by discussions around group dynamics and cooperation. This involves building up of a network of relationships among the students that extends beyond the gatherings. It involves the problems that arise from advice and counselling given about the form and content of the mini-projects. Alternating between gatherings and long periods during which one has time to work on one's own on the learning processes, constitutes the activity basis for the students' written progression. They are responsible for choosing which parts of their work they want to discuss with the advisor, and which parts they put out for collective discussion and criticism in the groups. They take responsibility for their own individual counselling needs and for thinking relationally about how the learning should progress in the plenary sessions of their groups. At the same time, however, there is a constant requirement for balance in the relationship between individual and collective needs.

Time pressure is a constant factor in the gatherings. People struggle over time, time in the groups versus time in individual counselling. Each student senses the need for balance such that they receive sufficient time to present their projects and that they have got feedback from the counsellor and fellow students. There may be competition about individual time with the counsellor, especially since the students write their individual thesis projects on their own, after a long period of group work, and the processes they go through are complex on many levels. As one student put it: 'The logic here is that our written work is private, and it's this that leaves its mark on us.'[79]

79 These processes are of course different during the four years. The question of time for concentrating in order to write up the thesis is very demanding during the last year. I often advise the students to try to get leave from their regular work for at least 6 months during the final year.

But one of the advantages of this way of organizing the learning in relationship to time is that the programme lasts four years. The students have time in between our joint sessions to reflect and grow. Liisa Torvinen (1997, 2003) has coined the concept 'A Student's Space' and asks if it is a prerequisite for activity and independence in learning.

## Counselling as Tailor-made Communication

Mentoring/counselling has become a very important concept in teacher education during the last decade. In general the term is thought of as a tool for enhancing reflective practice and upgrading the professionalism of schools. This is not what I want to focus on here; rather, I am concerned with the characteristic of the specific processes which take place when one helps people on the journey through higher education, the journey to create a written Masters thesis. The teacher is a leader for a group of students who work together; this teacher is also counselling each on her or his own individual project, often from the moment they start their Masters projects till they end it four years later.

The contact between students and teachers is marked by continuity and proximity. The advisory work is undertaken between gatherings by contacts conducted through the internet, postal service, fax and telephone. An important aspect of the counselling is to be accessible to the students' needs at the various phases of their work. For the advisor this means that setting aside time for the students and their needs is the primary feature of the teaching. This also means having empathy with the students' situation. The students require a rapid response in order to move forward. It is also important to make sure that the content of the teacher's response meets the students at the level of understanding they have reached. This form of counselling requires insight and understanding of the processes the students are going through. Some of the characteristics of counselling as a pedagogical activity are availability, consideration and personal engagement. An advisor is successful when her or his work is distinguished by tolerance for the unrefined and incomplete (Prestbakmo 1997, 31).

The individual counselling session is like an exercise in tailoring; it deals with developing the students' locked up ideas and potentials (Hovde 1995). The students go through big learning processes in the course of four years. This development is marked by many stages and various crises. It has to do with the integration of new knowledge, which often also changes the student's comprehension of society and their own place within it. It has to do with the development of new concepts in relation to how one experiences one's everyday life at school. One student commented:

> I see how important it is for my vocational training that I, who am going to engage in vocational training, have the knowledge of various theories and a scientific outlook. This is part of developing my repertoire; practical knowledge has become infinitely so much more than mere hammers and nails or syringes and bedpans. For me, practical knowledge has become an exciting composition where my outlook on both knowledge and humanity become the central nerve of that composition.

The counselling relationship is usually marked by the qualities of common human communication, and these relations can also be filled with contradictions. What is to be developed and stimulated by counselling is the desire for comprehension, not 'good relations' between advisor and student (Prestbakmo 1997, 70). In the context of counselling, the discussions between advisors and students are of great significance for how the students develop their own qualities of reflection. The aim of the counselling is to strengthen reflection such that the experiences the students have become as rich in learning as is possible. But this relationship is also one of power where the student is dependent upon the good will of the teacher. This raises complex questions about the 'asymmetrical' relationship between advisor and student.

## Learning through Activity and 'the Zone of Proximal Development'

The acquisition of knowledge in vocational pedagogy thesis-writing is built on a tradition of inductive learning and learning through activity, as discussed in Chapter 4. Activity theory deals with the relationship between society and the individual. It is an alternative social theory of knowledge which begins in the world of activity; the doings of actual people (see also Engestrøm 1986, 1996). Lev Vygotsky, highlighted the importance of everyday activities and everyday context in providing meaning; for him, this was central to the conceptual fabric for the schooling of the future. To make learning significant one must go beyond the classroom walls, beyond empty verbalism; real working knowledge grows through the analysis of multi-facetted everyday life. A further aspect has to do with the appropriation and mastery of mediational means, such as writing, assessed not only or necessarily through independent performance after guided practice, but by the ability of the students to participate in collaborate activities. The focus is, therefore is not in transferring skills as such, from those who know more to those who know less, but on the collaborative use of mediational means to create, obtain and communicate meaning. The learning processes depend on qualifying conversations that creates new inner dialogues in each individual by forcing them to grapple with material, concepts and associations that they are not yet familiar with. As one student commented, one learns a great deal from the problematic that occurs from having others participating in the group sessions.

But for the vocational teachers, these learning processes are also problematic. The work of another Russian scientist, Mikhail Bakhtin might bring us further in our understanding of the contradictions in the educational system, between the language of workshop learning and the academic classroom. His concept of 'speech genres' – the type of language used might shed light on the difficulty in bridging the gap between the everyday life of the vocations and of scientific and scholarly research. The experiences of the vocational teachers from their education and the manual labour market are often a working class experience; their world view and their construction of meaning are often in conflict with the hegemonic way of thinking. They speak another language. The complexity might be illustrated as follows: The kind of speech proper to the shop floor of a factory conflicts with that of the boardroom. Different social classes use the same words to signify different things, to summon up connotations common to their own class, but not necessarily so to other classes. The conversations between the world of the workshop teacher and the academic teacher can be like two ships passing in the night. These are some of the problems we encounter in the work of developing the field of vocational pedagogy in thesis work. But, in the words of Mikhail Bakhtin (1986, 1990), '[i]t is in the tension and confrontations between the different voices that new insight and understanding develop.'

Another perspective is that the psychological development of the individual is dependent upon the historical epoch in which the development occurs. Vygotsky associates A.R. Luria and A. Leontiev have further illuminated this phenomenon by showing the variation in the development of consciousness in relation to geographical conditions and social background (Mjelde and Daly 2000, Mjelde 1987, 1993). This point of view is of fundamental significance for all pedagogy and in this time of globalisation and development of information technology new challenges are unravelling before our very eyes.

## Conclusion

Regarding both form and content vocational teacher-training, is facing enormous changes and challenges. One of the problems in vocational teacher training has, moreover, been the division between learning a vocation and learning to teach. Vocational teachers have not had a formalized way to develop the vocational portion of their teacher training, something that is central to the new educational reforms. The new education for training vocational teachers, according to parliamentary White Paper 48 is based upon the following four points:

- The field of double practice; that is, the field of vocational competence and teaching competence.
- The vocational learning tradition and methods.
- Holism and continuity.
- Equivalence with other teacher education and other professionally oriented university and college education.

Anne-Lise Høstmark Tarrou (1995, 1997) discusses these dilemmas and shows that for more than the past three decades these four principles have been the expressed intention of many official documents central to the development of vocational education in Norway. But she also points out that 'at the very moment vocational training is included within the teaching system, together with the rest of the work of the school, the presumably implicit premises of literary culture are also laid down.' (1995, 61)

Some of the main questions that have arisen in the current situation are as follows. Will the vocational teacher education of the future come closer to a solution to these dilemmas by integrating vocational and pedagogical education in the three-year vocational teacher training programme? How can one maintain a relationship to learning in practice both in the labour market and in the teaching situation? In what way has the vocational pedagogical teaching model become fundamental to the development of learning and teaching, both in vocational teacher training and in the vocational fields of study in the secondary school system? How can one develop an understanding of the significance of the actualities of this form of learning in order to better understand all learning?

CHAPTER 10

# Workshop Learning and the Education of the Future

To sum up, the contradictions between the vocational learning tradition (workshop learning) and the academic learning tradition (classroom learning), learning in school and learning in workplaces, are at the core of the present educational reforms in upper secondary education (16- to-19-year-olds) in Norway as elsewhere in this time of globalization and social upheaval. A constant problem in the ongoing development of industry is the continuing need to recruit and train the workforce to fill the many and varied positions necessary for the current forms of production. With what kinds of skills should labour power be equipped? This is not a new problem. It has been on the agenda since the eve of industrialisation, as well as being at the centre of the discussion on this topic not only by Adam Smith but also by Karl Marx and Friedrich Engels (Mjelde 1987, 1994, 2004). The present stage in globalization and the changes in the modes of production with the new information and communication technology are challenging present divisions of labour and learning (Mjelde 2004, Roldan 2006).

In Norway, during the optimistic era of the 1960s, the slogan was that 'our future depends on how far we can raise the general level of education.' A slogan that arose in 'progressive pedagogical circles', was that students should 'learn for life' and not consider the labour market. The expansion and the reforms of the 1970s and 1980s was marked by structural reforms integrating different streams – at least rhetorically – but in upper secondary education the general and vocational streams continued to live their own relatively separate lives. The competition to enter the vocational field, whether in the upper secondary school or for an apprenticeship was fierce, and depended on the ebb and flow of the manual labour market. Between

50 % and 60 % of the youth cohort entered vocational education, but only a small proportion of them managed to obtain a craft certificate. Most of this youth cohort entered the labour market as semi-skilled and unskilled labour power. There was little evidence of 'equality through education'[80] (see Chapter 2, pp. 57–59).

These recurring problems were addressed indirectly in a series of official reports that came out in the late 1980s, and led to the enactment of Reform 94. Economic arguments were used: 'our wealth depends on our ability to produce and use knowledge. There is a connection between the growth in knowledge and the growth in the economy'[81] (NOU 1988, 7). 'The challenge for the Norwegian politics of knowledge is that it does not draw enough competence out of the talents of the population. The results we get are not good enough compared with the skills and abilities that can be developed.' The rhetoric alluded indirectly to class divisions within our supposedly classless society: 'This is not just a question about raising the performances for those with higher education; we need a better use of everyone's skills and abilities', said the sociologist and education minister, Gudmund Hernes, who was the mastermind behind Reform 94 (Skarpenes 2005).

A broad concept of knowledge for all and the creation of the holistic and integrated individual were the new goals of the 1990s. A new concept of knowledge and a new concept of the individual were needed. This is articulated in NOU 1991, 4: 'The society will need human beings who are creative and curious, who can act together,

80 These human beings are also the same hundreds of thousands who have gone in and out of adult education courses and rehabilitation centres during the past decades.

81 This is, of course, inspired by the development of the political economy of Europe. EU has made a strong impact on education in general and vocational education in particular, as a means of integrating the European labour market and making Europe stronger on the global market. A new European Qualification framework (EQF) is part of that effort. OECD has formulated reports on 'Knowledge and Skills for Life'; the Bologna and Lisbon declarations on adult education and life-long learning are important documents in this context. The Lisbon declaration set the goal to make Europe the most economically competitive region in the world by year 2010 (See also Antikainen 2005, Lindgren 2006).

who can be flexible and who satisfy demands about quality, order and discipline'.[82] The extremely rapid development of economic life actualized the question about the breadth and the depth of vocational education; moreover, the question of flexibility and 'learning to learn' was part of the curriculum. The students in Reform 94 were to take responsibility for their own life-long learning and keep abreast of the tasks of self-construction in the knowledge-based capitalistic society. Entrepreneurship should be at the core of the curriculum.

This emphasis on construction work continued with a general curriculum being developed as the prescription for all schooling: from kindergarten to the end of upper secondary school. The new curriculum plan, L-93, is divided into chapters with the following titles: 'The creative human being', 'the working human being', 'the meaning-seeking human being', 'the universally educated human being', 'the collaborative human being' and 'the environmental human being'. These are currently the mantras of the whole school system.

When one reads the preparatory documents for the reforms it sounds like the reformers have the famous passage of Karl Marx and Friedrich Engels in *The German Ideology* (1985: 53) in mind:

> For as soon as the distribution of labour comes into being, each man has an exclusive sphere of activity, which is forced upon him and from which he cannot escape. He is a hunter, a fisherman, a shepherd, or a critical critic, and must remain so if he does not want to lose his means of livelihood; while in communist society, where nobody has one exclusive sphere of activity but each can become accomplished in any branch he wishes, society regulates the general production and thus makes it possible for me to do one thing today and another tomorrow, to hunt in the morning, to fish in the afternoon, rear cattle in the evening, criticise after dinner, just as I have a mind, without ever becoming hunter, fisherman, shepherd or critic.

82 A digression, but to the point; this is what the development of the productive forces demands in certain sectors today, but the development is not without contradictions. As a Danish employer said in the 1980s: 'We need young people who can act and think independently and who do what they are told.' (see Mjelde 1993, 62).

The social division of labour in the formation of the industrial class society and the relationship between hand and mind as it had developed in general through history, and under industrial capitalism in particular, was the centre of the concern for Karl Marx both in *Capital* (1867) and in his philosophical works. Marx was particularly concerned with how the division of labour divided thought from feeling, theory from practice. The writings of Karl Marx attempt to present the theme of school and work from both theoretical and practical viewpoints. Marx formulated the concept of combining theory and practice to provide training for a genuine understanding of the various forms of modern production. Marx was inspired by the polytechnic training he saw in the emerging society around him. Polytechnic training represented an education for one class to meet the specific needs and further the interests of another class, the bourgeoisie. Marx, however, went on to argue that a polytechnic education also had a more general aim; this form of education in his view, properly embedded in society's production processes , was the only way to produce fully developed, well rounded human beings.[83] Marx discusses what kind of education would bring about this formation of the individual in a future society. He thought the answer lay in recent developments of his time, some of which allowed him to see 'the germs of the education of the future' (Marx 1967, 483; see also Mjelde 1987, 1995). He paid special attention to the schools of craft training developed in France after the 1848 revolution, which attempted to establish a type of secondary education different from the academic kind provided by the lycées. This speaks directly to the contradictions we can observe in the development between old traditions, between the ideology and the pedagogical model of the old gymnasiums and the traditions as they have developed in vocational education and in the apprenticeship traditions. As I have pointed out in preceding chapters, the goal for Norwegian education was to further integrate vocational and general education. I have tried to unravel some of the complexities found in these efforts. My viewpoint has

83 When we see the rhetoric in the latest reforms in Norwegian education, where one of the goals is to create 'holistic and integrated individuals', one can only wonder where the inspiration has come from.

been quite explicitly the standpoint of the working class and the contradictions this class, with its currently limited power and influence, faces when it comes to vocational education.

Reform 94 was implemented at the speed of lightning in 1994. The old apprenticeship school was abolished and now *everyone*, whether they liked it or not, was going to enter the upper secondary school for two additional years of mostly classroom work, and then the 'everybody' cohort would bifurcate, going either on to university studies, or into two years of apprenticeship in one or other of the vocational fields. In the vocational line, they were to enter at 16 and finish at 19. Specialised vocational education was to decrease and general classroom education, increase during these first two years of the programme. Vocational education expanded into new fields, and gave many youngsters new opportunities for becoming skilled labour, particularly in the caring professions. The apprenticeship system was strengthened and 150,000 youngsters now participate in apprenticing schemes. But the changes have also created astonishing dropout problems, a dropout rate of 39% for the girls and 46% for the boys in the vocational fields. More girls than boys complete upper secondary school within the allotted time. These differences are found both in the academic and the vocational streams. In the academic field, 86% of the girls and 80% of the boys complete the programme requirements within a five year time period. Corresponding numbers in the vocational field are 61% of the girls and 54% of the boys (Central Bureau of Statistics 2004, White Paper No 30 2003–2004)[84].

The situation is ripe with contradictions. Today, new challenges face both vocational training and general education. The vocational field has always been related to working life, but the general knowledge components of these programmes are often presented without relevance to the students' everyday lives; similarly, the general edu-

84 We have seen a strong improvement in official statistical registration of vocational education during the last years. Of course this lays the groundwork for getting an overall view of the situation in education. Before the present reforms statistics on vocational training and apprenticeship were made by a separate body, the National Council for Vocational Training in Working Life and there was no coordination with the educational statistics of the Norwegian Bureau of Statistics.

cation lacks a relation to work and the curriculum is usually presented in fragments or even modules. After the present reforms we have seen the downgrading of old traditional workshop in the vocational field and an expansion of general subjects. We have seen a revival and expansion of apprenticeship programmes. We have seen an increase in dropout problems on the one hand but also, on the other, an expansion of vocational education into new fields giving working class girls new opportunities on the labour market (Utdanningsspeilet 2005).

In recent decades, developments on the labour market and in family policy (e.g. two-income families, day care possibilities, and stress on domestic gender equity) have challenged traditional gender patterns, especially as related to vocational training within the school system. *Reform 94* has made concrete the question of the man's role and the woman's role, and the question of the right and duty to work and to take up the nurturing and caring tasks in family and society. The integration of learning at school and learning at work are discussed at a higher level than ever before. New concepts have arisen in the discourse on learning and teaching. A shift has taken place from teaching to learning. Questions about what is practice and what is theory in learning situations are being discussed.

New fundamental questions have also been posed in the social organisation of knowledge. The feminist movement, for instance, has raised the remoteness of much of social research from people's everyday life. In the everyday life that we human beings live, the lived situation is a chain of dialectical processes: Experience lays the basis for knowledge; theory gives breadth of understanding to practice; thinking informs activity; and activity informs thinking. These processes occur in human beings *in their relatedness*, which is, steered by historically specific values and the structures of society (Gaskell 1992, Smith 1987). People's everyday world as problematic is discussed as a core in the education system. Experiential learning, reflection and scientific thinking are on the agenda. Despite the constant pressure for vocational education to assist market relations, science by the people and for the people, and a pedagogy that has these perspectives as its starting point, is at least one of the trends being promoted as necessary to the future of the Norwegian education system. This gives hope for pedagogy for the people.

# Conclusion

The relationship between the conceptual world of academic education, untouched by the realities of the practical world, and the practice-centred world of vocational education, with its roots in actual work (though usually work that is not linked reflectively to the precise laws of science upon which the practical activity is based) is a classic theme both in the sociology of knowledge and in educational policy. Alfred Sohn Rethel makes the following statement in his important book: *Intellectual and Manual Labour. A Critique of Epistemology*:

> Admittedly it must be taken into consideration that the philosophical tradition is itself a product of the division between mental and manual labour, and since the beginning with Pythagoras, Heraclitus and Parmides has been a preserve of intellectuals for intellectuals, inaccessible to manual workers (Sohn-Rethel 1978, 18).

The development of the educational school systems and the relation between class and vocational and general education has made these contradictions more visible; moreover the new qualification demands on the manual labour market challenge the strong divisions of the past. This is not necessarily because there has been any theoretical clarification about the relation between these two traditions, but rather, by way of recognizing that a radical technological development has changed the content and the organization of work. The question of the broader integration of vocational and general education has taken on the colouring of a political question. The New European Qualification Framework and the question of the free movement of labour are closely connected to the 'European Nation building' project and its competitive goals on the world market (OECD 2003, 2004, a,b,c). This is one of the factors driving the integration of the various elements to make the educational process more effective. This is not necessarily because there has been any theoretical clarification about the relation between these two teaching traditions, but rather, by way of recognizing that a radical technological development has changed the content and the organization of the work. This is what makes it necessary to integrate the various elements to make the educational process more effective. This is not a new difficulty. 'Learning by doing' is one of the methods pedagogues have used to try to solve the contradictions within the school systems of the twentieth century. In the USA, John Dewey laid down the basis for the reform movement on such a foundation (Dewey&Dewey 1915), as did Celestin Freinet with his presses in France (1975), and Georg Kerschensteiner with his 'Lehrwerkstatte' (workplace learning) in Germany (see Mjelde 1996a).[85] In their reform activities, all three had different scientific starting points, as well as different goals, but workshop learning is common to them all, and central to their thinking about how education ought to be organized.

In terms of being able to bridge these traditional divisions, between works of hand and work of mind, between practice and theory and between vocational and general education there is a promising new interest in and understanding of these dichotomies. In recent years, researchers from several different disciplines in the Nordic countries have set themselves the goal of working towards more inclusive education and synthesizing theory around vocational pedagogy, where different methods of thinking about learning are front and centre (Halvorsen&Olsen 1992, Halvorsen 1994, Heikkinen 1994, 1995, Hiim&Hippe 2001, Nielsen&Kvale, 1999, 2003, Mjelde &Tarrou 1992, Mjelde 1993, 1994a&b, 1996a&b, Årkrog 2003). Even though the researchers who have been at the core of this field use different concepts, they all have a 'sense of praxis as their starting point' (Halvorsen 1994, 119). Concepts such as 'praxis theory' (Handel&Lauvås 1983), 'tacit knowledge' (Polanyi 1983), 'the reflexive practitioner' (Schøn 1983), and 'activity knowledge' (Molander 1993) seem to have inspired research work in vocational pedagogy. Tor Halvorsen writes: 'Perhaps future research in vocational education and working life will establish knowledge that shows the ideal paradigm of the unified school is atypical when seen in a historical light, despite the hegemony that this cultural inheritance has today' (1994, 123).

85 Progressive pedagogy also has strong roots in Norway. Anna Sethne and Olav Storstein (see Storstein 1973) are central names here from the inter-war years of the twentieth century.

To separate academic thinking from practical life is as damaging as separating practical life from academic matters. Given the way the educational system has developed to the present, we have a situation where both general academic and vocational education separate knowledge from experience, theory from practice, thought from action. A course of studies that takes into account all these factors and incorporates heart and brain, conceptualisation processes, and their practical exercise, is necessary for a better education for all. Similarly, a working life wherein one can advance with experience and maturity, where the mechanic can become an engineer, and the caregiver with a craft certificate can, stone by stone, build her/himself into a nurse, radiographer, or doctor, is essential if we are to achieve a better life for all (see also Freire 1998).

Contradictions in the present-day school show the limitations that sectional interests in society create when one tries to use the school and education as an instrument for bringing about social change. In other words, one comes up against the interests of the powerful and the conventional social boundaries when one tries to create both a common school and conformity through education – especially in a society that is not nearly as equal and united as the politicians assure us it is. To clarify the contradictions as they appear in the curricula of the vocational trades in the upper secondary school is not to deny that some are better than others. It is important to put forward an understanding of both sides of this human activity, both the practical workshop tradition and the scholarly general educational route. They should both be taken up, but in such a manner that encourages them to enrich one another. Contradictions can also be made fruitful insofar as they are analysed openly and plainly, made conscious and comprehensible, and thus capable of contributing to wider democratisation of the school and education in general through development of pedagogy for all.

Lev Vygotsky: 'Neither Hand nor Mind can do much Alone. The deed is brought to fruition through Activity and Cooperation.'

Figure 10: 'Education for the Future: Work of Hand and Mind and Stored Experience' (book).
Building site: Fritsøe brygge, Larvik, in April 2003.
Part of Education Project: 'School and Work Place'.
Teacher and Photographer: Jan Thore Karlsen.

# Bibliography

## General

Austenaa, M. 2005. Er fagutdanningen på ville veier. In Oslo: *El-Magasinet*, pp.31–41.

Aamodt, P. O. & E. Brandt. 1982. Jenters yrkesutdanning. Veien til likestilling i arbeidslivet? Oslo *Videregående opplæring* 5/6, pp. 21–31.

Aarkrog, V. 2003. Læring i detaljhandel. In K. Nielsen & S. Kvale (eds.), *Praktikkens læringslandskap. At lære gjennom arbejde* Copenhagen: Akademisk forlag.

Aarebrot, R. 1991. Finsk skolereform fra Koskenniemi til i dag med særlig henblikk på de praktiske fag (Doctoral dissertation). Copenhagen: University of Copenhagen.

Aftenposten [Oslo daily newspaper], Sept 3, 1980.

Antikainen, A. 2005. Between Empowerment and Control: A State Intervention into Participation in Adult Education in Finland. In *European Education* Vol. 37 (2), pp. 21–31.

Andersen, E. 1984. Norsk yrkesopplæring 1890–1940. Masters thesis. Oslo: Statens Yrkespedagogiske Høgskole (SYH).

Andersgård, I. 1983. Settersker og typografer – splittelse mellom kvinner og menn. In I. Blom (ed.), *Kvinner selv*, pp. 22–46. Oslo: Universitetsforlaget.

Annfelt, T. 1988. Utdanning, Normer og verdier: En analyse av verdiformidlingen i hustellfaglig lærerutdanning. (Masters thesis). Oslo: University of Oslo, Pedagogisk forskningsinstitutt.

Applebaum, H. 1992. *The Concept of Work: Ancient, Medieval and Modern. New York: State University of* New York Press.

Askerøi, E. & M. Høie. 1992. Om generative sosiale mønster i undervisning av forskning. In L. Mjelde & A-L. H. Tarrou (eds.), *Arbeidsdeling i en brytningstid: Yrkespedagogiske utfordringer i skole og arbeidsliv*, pp. 160–172. Oslo: Ad Notam Gyldendal.

Askerøi, E. & M. Høie. 1999. *Les og lær? Lærebokas rolle i yrkesfag.* Oslo: Tano, Aschehoug.

Avis, J. 1995. The Validation of Learner Experience, A Conservative Practice? *Studies in the Education of Adults* 27(2), pp. 173–186.

Axelsson, A. 1989. *Upper Secondary School in Retrospect: The View of Former Students.* Uppsala: Acta Universitatis Upsaliensis

Bakhtin, M. 1981. *The Dialogic Imagination: Four Essays.* Austin: University of Texas Press.

Bakhtin, M. 1986. *Speech Genres and Other Late Essays*. Austin: University of Texas Press.
Baran, A. 1987. Contested Terrain Revisited: Technology and Gender Definitions of Work in the Printing Industry 1850–1920. In B. Wright (ed.), *Women, Work and Technology*, Ann Arbor, MI: University of Wisconsin Press.
Barrett, M. & A. Phillips, eds. 1992. *Destabilizing Theory*. Cambridge: Polity Press.
Båtnes, P. 1995. En modell for lærebokstudiet. Lærebøkenes danningsidealer som normsettere for kunnskapsformidling. In E. B. Johnsen (ed.), *Virkelighetens forvaltere*, pp. 92–108. Oslo: Universitetsforlaget.
Becker, H. 1986. *Doing Things Together: Selected Papers*. Evanston, IL: Northwestern University Press.
Beechey, V. 1987. *Unequal Work*. London: Verso Press.
Berg, T. 1999. Norskbøker i yrkesfaglige studieretninger – fins de egentlig? *Norsklæreren*, No. 2., 1999, pp. 21–26.
Berg, T. & E. Lauritsen. 1999. Elektro mellom læring i skole og arbeidsliv. (Masters thesis). Akershus: Høgskolen i Akershus.
Bergli, T. 1995. *Reform og innsats 94/95*. Akershus: Høgskolen i Akershus.
Bergli, T. 1997. *Fire studieretninger i andre reformår*. Akershus: Høgskolen i Akershus.
Bergli, T. & E. Frøyland. 1995. *Reform 94: Plan og praksis*. Akershus: Høgskolen i Akershus.
Berner, B. 1989. *Kunskapens vägar. Teknikk och lärande i skola och arbetsliv*. Lund: Archiv förlag.
Billett, S. 2000. Co-participation at Work: Knowing and Working Knowledge. In D. Boud & C. Symes (eds.), *Working Knowledge: Productive Learning at Work*, pp. 29–36. Sydney: National University of Technology (NTU).
Bjerketvedt, F., E. Heltorp & L. Mjelde. 1971. *Et undervininingstilbud tilpasset elevenes behov. Om organisatorisk og pedagogisk differensiering*. Oslo: Sogn Yrkeskole.
Bjørnavold, J, M. Dahlstrøm & T. Skinningsrud. 1995. *Fagopplæring i arbeidslivet og Reform 94*, Pt. 1 & 2. Tromsø: Norut.
Blichfeldt, J. F. 1992. Om kompetanse og kunnskapsutvikling. In L. Mjelde & A-L. H. Tarrou (eds.), *Arbeidsdeling I en brytningstid – Yrkespedagogiske utfordringer i skole og arbeidsliv*, pp. 42–55. Oslo: Ad Notam Gyldendal.
Blichfeldt, J. F. et al 1996. *Utdanning for alle?* Oslo: Tano. Aschehoug.
Bongo, M. 1998. Yrkesrettet voksenopplæring i reformtid. (Masters thesis). Akershus: Høgskolen i Akershus.
Bongo, M. 2001a. Videregående opplæring: Møtestedet mellom to læringstradisjoner. Kan en av reformproblemene tilskrives å ha grunnlaget i de grunnleggende motsetninger mellom ulike læringstradisjoner? Conference paper, Høgskolen i Akershus, 31 October, 2001.
Bongo, M. 2001b. Notes from personal communication with Liv Mjelde.
Boud, D. & C. Symes (eds.) 2000. *Working Knowledge: Productive Learning at Work*. Sydney: National University of Technology (NTU).

Bratteli, T. 1946. *Ungdommen og samfunnet.* Oslo: Arbeidernes ungdomsfylking.
Braverman, H. 1974. *Labour and Monopoly Capital: The Degradation of Work in the Twentieth Century.* New York and London: Monthly Review Press.
Bridenthal, R., A. Grossmann & M Kaplan 1984. *When Biology Became Destiny: Women in Weimar and Nazi Germany.* New York : Monthly Review Press
Browne, K. 1981. Schooling, Capitalism and the Mental/Manual Division of Labour. *Sociological Review* 29(3), pp. 445–473.
Brox, O. 1990. Sosial lagdeling, fattigdom, dyd og belønning 1890–1990. *Samtiden* No. 3, pp. 2–10.
Bruner, J. 1963a. *The Process of Education* New York: Vintage Books.
Bruner, J. 1963b. *On Knowing: Essays for the Left Hand.* Cambridge, MA: The Belknap Press of Harvard University.
Bruner, J. 1983. *In Search of Mind. Essays in Autobiography.* New York: Harpers Colophon Books.
Bruner, J. 1996. *The Culture of Education.* Cambridge, MA: Harvard University Press.
Castro, C. de Moura & R. de Quadros Carvalho 1985. *Automation in Brazil: Who's Afraid of Digital Circuits?* Tunisia: UNESCO.
Cavendish, R. 1982. *Women on the Line.* London: Routledge & Kegan Paul.
Charlot, B. 1987. *L'école en mutation: Crise de l'école et mutations socials.* Paris: Payot.
Christensen, D. 1887. Fra en moder til mødre [From a Mother to Mothers]. (Unpublished manuscript) Akershus: Høgskolen i Akershus
Christensen, D. 1891. *Kogebog for folkeskolen og hjemmet.* Kristiania: J. W. Cappelen Forlag.
Christensen, D. & H. Helgesen. 1894. *Kogebok for folkeskolen og hjemmet.* Kristiania: self-published.
Christiansen, L. L. 1998. *Bevisste utdanningsvalg.* Oslo: Ministry of Church, Education and Research
Cockburn, C. 1983. *Brothers, Male Dominance and Technological Change.* London: Pluto Press.
Cockburn, C. 1985. *Machinery of Dominance: Women, Men and Technical Know-how.* London: Pluto Press.
Cockburn, C. 1986. The Material of Male Power. In *Waged Work, A Reader* (edited by *Feminist Review*), pp. 93–113. London: Virago Press.
Cohen, S. & J. Zysman. 1987. *Manufacturing Matters: The Myth of Post-Industrial Economy.* New York: Basic Books.
Coy, M. W. 1989. *Apprenticeship: From Theory to Method and Back Again.* Albany: State University of New York Press.
Daly, R. & L. Mjelde. 2000. Learning at the Point of Production: New Challenges in the Social Division of Knowledge. In D. Boud & C. Symes (eds.), *Working Knowledge: Productive Learning at Work*, pp. 105–112. Sydney: National University of Technology (NTU).

Damasio, A. 1999. *The Feeling of What Happens: Body and Emotions in the Making of Consciousness*. London: Heinemann.
Davin, A. 1982. Child Labour, the Working Class Family and Domestic Ideology in Nineteenth Century Britain. *Development and Change* 13, pp. 633–652.
Dewey, J. 1900. *School and Society*. Chicago: University of Chicago Press.
Dewey, J. 1916. *Democracy and Education* Toronto: Collier-Macmillan.
Dewey, J. & E. Dewey. 1915. *Schools of Tomorrow*. London: J. M. Dent & Sons.
Dreyfus, H. & S. Dreyfus. 1986. *Mind over Machine*. New York: The Free Press.
Drevvatne, P. 1983. Faculty Interaction and Cooperation: A Field Study in a Norwegian High School (Dissertation). University of California at Santa Barbara.
Drevvatne, P. & B. Johnsen. 1976. *Studiebok i pedagogikk for yrkeslærere*. Oslo: Universitetsforlaget.
Dyrdal, A. 1995. Teori og praksis – i praksis. Paper presented at the 1995 Work and Literature Seminar, Høgskolen i Akershus.
Ellingsæter, A. L. 1995a. Ulikhet I det postindustrielle samfunn: Klasse, kjønn og generasjon. *Sosiologisk tidsskrift* No 3, pp. 263–283.
Ellingsæter, A. L. 1995b. *Gender, Work and Social Change: Beyond Dualistic Thinking*. ISF Report 95–14. Oslo: Institutt for Samfunnsforskning.
Ellingsæter, A. L. 1999. Dual Breadwinners between State and Market. In R. Crompton (ed.), *Restructuring Gender Relations and Employment: The Decline of the Male Breadwinner*, pp. 40–59. Oxford: Oxford University Press.
Ellingsæter, A. L. T. Noack & M. Rønsen 1997. Sosial ulikhet blant kvinner. Polarisering, utjevning eller status quo? *Tidsskrift for samfunnsforskning* N 38, pp. 33–69.
Ellingsæter, A. L. & J. Rubery. 1997. Gender Relations and the Norwegian Labour Market Model. In J. E. Dølvik & A. Steen (eds.), *Making Solidarity Work? The Norwegian Labour Market Model in Transition*, pp. 111–151. Oslo: Scandinavian University Press.
Enerstvedt, R. 1987. *Virksomhet og mening: Utviklingen av læremotivasjon hos norske skolebarn*. Oslo: University of Oslo, Institutt for Sosiologi.
Engen, T. O. 1992. *Fagopplæring i arbeidslivet. Egenart, status og satsningsområder*. Hamar: Oplandske Bokforlag.
Engestrøm,Y & P. Hakkarainen 1981. Is Scientific Instruction Possible? In *Tidskrift for Nordisk Forening for Pedagogisk Forskning* No. 2, pp. 8–26.
Engestrøm, Y 1986 Editorial: Work, learning and activity. *Nordisk Pedagogik Vol. 6 (1), p. 1.*
Engestrøm, Y. 1996. Development Work Research as Educational Research: Looking Back Ten Years into the Zone of Proximal Development. *Nordisk pedagogikk* 16 (3), pp. 131–142.
Enkenberg, J. 1994. Situated Cognition and Cognitive Apprenticeship: New Frameworks for Education of Professional Skills. In A. Heikkinen, (ed.), *Vocational Education and Culture: European Perspectives from History and Life History*, pp. 204–216. Tampere: University of Tampere Press.

Faag, Å. 1997. Følelser og yrkespedagogikk. Masters thesis. Akershus: Høgskolen i Akershus.

Flaaten, S. V. 1999. Bedriften som arena for læring, opplæring og sosialisering. En sosiologisk undersøkelse av fagopplæring ved Hydro Industripark. Masters thesis in sociology, University of Bergen.

Flyvberg, B. 1991. *Rationalitet og magt: Det konkretes vitenskap*. Odense: Akademisk forlaget.

Fokuyama, F. 1997. *The End of Order*. London: Social Market Foundation.

Forsøksrådet for skoleverket 1973: Rapport om forsøk i videregående opplæring. Oslo.

Foucault, M. 1979. *The History of Sexuality*. Hammondsworth: Penguin Books.

Freinet, C. 1975. *Folkets skole*. Oslo: Pax forlag.

Freire, P. 1998. *Pedagogy of the Heart*. New York: Continuum Publishing Company.

Gaskell, J. 1992. *Gender Matters from School to Work*. Toronto: OISE Press, University of Toronto.

Gaskell, J. 1995. Making It Work: Gender and Vocational Education. In J. Gaskell & J. Willinsky (eds.), *Gender In/Forms Curriculum: From Enrichment to Transformation,* pp. 59–76. Toronto: OISE Press, University of Toronto.

Glassmann, M. 2001. Dewey and Vygotsky: Society, Experience and Inquiry in Educational Practice. *Educational Researcher* 30 (4), pp. 3–14.

Glucksmann, M. 1995. Gender and the 'Total Social Organisation of Labour'. *Gender, Work and Organization*, Vol 2, No 2, pp. 63–75.

Goody, E. 1989. Learning, Apprenticeship and the Division of Labour. In M. W. Coy, ed., *Apprenticeship: From Theory to Method and Back Again*, pp. 233–256. Albany, NY: State University of New York Press.

Grignon, C. 1971. *L'Ordre des choses*. Paris: Editions de Minuit.

Grimestad, V. 1993. Om bakgrunn og prestasjoner: Elever med grunnlag i forkurs mekaniske fags utvikling med hensyn til trivsel, motivasjon og sosial integrering i læremessig sammenheng. Masters thesis, Oslo: Statens Yrkespedagogiske Høgskole (SYH).

Grosjean, G. 2001. The Social Organization of Learning: Educational Provision, Process and Outcomes. Paper presented at the Western Research Network on Education and Training 5th Annual Conference "Connecting It All: Linking Economics, Education and Policy." Faculty of Education, University of British Columbia, Vancouver, March 30–31, 2001.

Grønbæk-Hansen, K. 1993. Kvalifisering til maskulinitet og underordning. De maskuline bastioner i erhvervsuddannelserne. In Nielsen A.M. et al (eds.), *Køn i forandring,* pp. 212–224. København: Forlaget Hyldespjæt.

Grønseth, E. 1975. Work–Sharing Families. *Acta Sosiologica* 18 (1–2): 202–221.

Gulbrandsen, A 1994. Paradigmeskifte i lærerutdanningen. *Norsk Pedagogisk Tidskrift No 2,* pp. 66–78.

Haga, T. & S. Michelsen. 1993. Fra fagmann til yrkespedagog. Om yrkesskolens undervisningsformer og lærernes yrkesbevissthet. Gruppen for flerfaglig arbeidslivsforskning, University of Bergen, *Arbeid, Historie og Samfunn (AHS) Serie b, 1993–2.*

Halvorsen, T. 1994. Forskning om yrkesutdanning og arbeidsliv. In J. Lauglo (ed.), *Norsk forskning om utdanning: Perspektiver og veivalg*, pp. 96–126. Oslo: Ad Notam Gyldendal.

Halvorsen, T. & O. Olsen 1992. *Det kvalifiserte samfunn?* Oslo: Ad Notam Gyldendal.

Hammer, T. E. Ravndal & P. Vaglum 1985. *Arbeid istedenfor rus.* Oslo: Universitetsforlaget.

Handal, G. & P. Lauvås 1983. *På egne vilkår.* Oslo: Cappelen.

Hargreaves, D. 1982: *The Challenge for the Comprehensive School, Culture, Curriculum, Community.* London: Routledge & Kegan P.

Harris, K. 1979. *Education and Knowledge.* London: Routledge & Kegan Paul.

Harris, R., P. Willis & M. Simons 1999 *Learning the Job: Juggling the Messages in On-and-Off-the-Job Training.* Adelaide: NCVER Press.

Harney, K. et al. (eds.) 2002. *Lifelong Learning: One Focus, Different Systems.* Frankfurt am Main. Peter Lang.

Heikkinen A. et al (eds.) 1994. *Vocational Education and Culture: European Perspectives from History and Life History.* Hämeenlinna: University of Tampere Press.

Heikkinen A. et al (eds.) 1995. *Vocational Education in the Future.* Hämeenlinna: University of Tampere Press.

Heikkinen A. et al (eds.) 1997. *Apprenticeship in Europe: Toward the Year 2000.* Hämeenlinna: University of Tampere Press.

Heikkinen A. et al (eds.) 1999. *Work of Hands and Work of Minds in Times of Change.* Jyvæskyla: University of Jyvæskyla Press.

Heinz, W. 2001. Transitions to Employment in a Cross-national Perspective. Paper presented at the Western Research Network on Education and Training 5th Annual Conference: "Connecting It All: Linking Economics, Education and Policy." Faculty of Education, University of British Columbia, Vancouver, March 30–31, 2001.

Helgesen, H. 1914. Folkeskolekjøkkener. In M. Høgh & F. Mørck (eds.), *Norske kvinner: En oversigt av deres stilling og livsvilkaar i hundredaaret 1814–1914*, pp. 197–203. Kristiania: Berg & Høgh's forlag.

Helgesen, H. 1928. *Skolekjøkkenundervisningen.* Oslo: H. Aschehoug & Co.

Henriksson, L. 2001. Gendering the Theories of Professions – Five Narratives. In P. Gonon, K. Haefel, A. Heikkinen, I. Ludwig (eds.), *Gender Perspectives on Vocational Education,* pp. 305–330. Bern: Peter Lang.

Hernes, G. 1974. *Om ulikhetens reproduksjon. I forskningens lys.* Oslo: NAVF's anniversary book.

Hernes, G. 2001. De mest spennende ideer. Tilbakeblikk på et reformtiår. In H. Harning (ed.), *Årbok for Norsk utdanningshistorie.* Notodden: Telemarksforskning.

Hernes, G. & K. Knudsen. 1976. *Om utdanning og ulikhet. Levekårsundersøkelsen.* Oslo: NOU No. 46.
Hertaas, E. W. 1990. Studieavbrudd, omfang og årsaker. Masters Thesis. SYH .
Hiim, H. & E. Hippe. 1992. Vurdering av en didaktisk strategi for yrkeslærerutdanning. In L. Mjelde & A-L. H.Tarrou (eds.), *Arbeidsdeling i en brytningstid:Yrkespedagogiske utfordringer i skole og arbeidsliv*, pp. 111–133. Oslo: Ad Notam Gyldendal.
Hiim, H. & E. Hippe. 2001. *Å utdanne profesjonelle yrkesutøvere: Yrkesdidaktikk og yrkeskunnskap.* Oslo: Gyldendal.
Holck, M. 2001. Kjemi som støttefag. En analyse av kjemi som støttefag ved høgre profesjonsutdanninger, med spesiell vekt på faglærerutdanningen i ernæring, helse og miljø. Doctoral dissertation, Oslo: University of Oslo, Det utdanningsvitenskapelige fakultet.
Hovde, S. 1995 Veiledning som skreddersydd kommunikasjon. Unpublished manuscript. Oslo Institute of Sociology, University of Oslo.
Høst, H. 1997a. Konstruksjon av omsorgsarbeideren. Masters thesis. *Arbeid, Historie og Samfunn (AHS) Serie A, 1997–2.* Bergen.
Høst, H. 1997b. Konstruksjon av omsorgsarbeideren i spenningsfeltet mellom utdanningspolitikk, kommunalisering og interesseorganisering. *Arbeid, Historie og Samfunn (AHS)*: Gruppe for flerfaglig forskning. Bergen: University of Bergen.
Høst, H. & O. Skarpenes. 2000. Fagopplæring i småbedrifter under nye vilkår. *Arbeid, Historie og Samfunn (AHS) Serie B.* Bergen: University of Bergen.
Handverk og Industri No.4, 1983.
Illeris, K. 1999. *Læring – aktuell læringsteori i spenningsfeltet mellom Piaget, Freud og Marx.* Roskilde Universitetsforlaget.
Isachsen, S. 2000. *At forferdige en selskapskjole eller en spaserdrakt: Tradisjoner og forandringer i håndverksfagene.* Oslo: Yrkeslitteratur.
Jackson, N. 1992. Rethinking Vocational Knowledge. (Unpublished paper presented 1992 at Statens Yrkespedagogisk Høgskole, Oslo).
Jangård, Hilde (1978: Er skolen på kollisjonskurs med arbeiderkulturen? In L. Monsen (ed.) *Kunnskapsosiologi og skoleutvikling,* pp. 99–116. Oslo: Universitetsforlaget.
Jarvis, P. 1987. Meaningful and Meaningless Experience: Towards an Analysis of Learning from Life. *Adult Education Quarterly* 37 (3), pp. 164–172.
Jensen, S. 1997. Kvinner og kvinnekamp i arbeid og fagforening. In T. A. Johnsen (ed.). *Fra bly til bytes: Oslo grafiske fagforening 1872–1997*, pp. 87–140. Oslo: Oslo Grafiske fagforening.
Jenson, J. 1988. The Talents of Women, the Skills of Men: Flexible Specialisation and Women. In S. Wood (ed.), *The Degradation of Work.* London: Hutchinson.
Jenson, J. E. Hagen & C. Reddy. 1988. *Feminisation of the Labour Force: Paradoxes and Promises.* Cambridge: Polity Press.
Johnsen, Anna-Clara Eden 1986. *100 års ensomhet. Faget heimkunnskap i sosialpedagogisk perspektiv.* Kristiansand: Kristiansand Lærerskole.

Kaarinen, M. 1994. The Vocational Education of Girls in Finland 1917–1939. In A. Heikkinen (ed.), *Vocational Education and Culture: European Prospects from History and Life History,* pp. 177–188. Hämeenlinna: University of Tampere Press.

Kløve, B. 1993. Trøste og bære, nødvendig å lære. Masters thesis. Oslo: Statens Yrkespedagogiske Høgskole (SYH).

Kokkersvold, E. & L. Mjelde 1982. *Yrkeskolen som forsvant.* Oslo: Gyldendal.

Kornes, O. 1990. On the Social Construction of the Industrial Skilled Worker. *Arbeid, Historie og Samfunn (AHS) serien.* Bergen: University of Bergen.

Kristiania Håndverk og Industriforening. 1907. Innstilling av 1906.

Kvale, S. 1993. En pædagogisk rehabilitering av mesterlæren? *Dansk pædagogisk tidsskrift* 41 (1), pp. 9–18.

Kvalsund, R., J. O. Myklebust & F. O. Båtevik. 1998. *Når vilkår varierer – særskild tilrettelegging i videregående opplæring: Gjennomgående mønster.* Volda: Møreforskning.

Langli, Leif 1995 (Personal communication during a course given by Liv Mjelde, entitled "Vocational Pedagogy and the Social Organisation of Knowledge").

Lave, J. & E. Wenger 1991. *Situated Learning.* Cambridge: Cambridge University Press.

Lee, D. J. 1981. Skill, Class and Craft: A Theoretical Critique and a Critical Case. *Sociology* 15, pp. 57–77.

Leithe, T. 1995. Skolebasert yrkesutdanning: Barne- og ungdomsarbeiderfaget etter Reform 94. Examination project, Akershus: Høgskolen i Akershus Yrkespedagogisk institutt.

Leithe, T. 1997. Skolebasert yrkesutdanning: Barne- og ungdomsarbeiderfaget etter Reform 94. Masters thesis. Akershus: Høgskolen i Akershus Yrkespedagogisk institutt.

Leontiev, A. N. 1978. *Activity, Consciousness and Personality.* Englewood Cliffs NJ: Prentice Hall.

Lesjö, J. H. 1979. Fra Gutenberg til Bloksberg. Masters thesis. Oslo: University of Oslo Institute of Sociology.

Lien, T. 1984. *Kvalifisering til arbeid: En analyse av teori og praksis på et arbeidsmarkedskurs.* Trondheim: Norsk Voksenpedagogisk Institutt.

Lien, T. 1991. Om læringstradisjon og yrkespedagogisk kompetanseutvikling. Paper. Oslo: Statens Yrkespedagogiske Høgskole (SYH).

Lien, T. 1995. *Men helst vil jeg ha en jobb: Evaluering av AMO-kurs i Vestfold.* Fylkesarbeidskontoret i Vestfold.

Lien, T & L. Mjelde 1999. From Job to Education, from Education to Job in A. Heikkinen et al (eds.) *Work of Hands and Work of Minds in Times of Change,* pp. 43–56. Jyvæskyla: University of Jyvæskyla.

Liljeström, R. 1979. *Kultur och arbete.* Stockholm: Liber förlag.

Lindbekk, T 1973. Skolesosiologi. Oslo: Tapir.

Lindblad, S. 1997. Learning about Late Modernity. Notions on Teachers' Work, Youth Cultures and Restructuring of Education in Sweden. Oslo: Pact meeting 19–22 of May.

Lindgren, A. 2001. Male and Female Identities in Higher Vocational Education in Sweden. In P. Gonon, K. Haefel, A. Heikkinen, I. Ludwig (eds.) *Gender Perspectives on Vocational Education*, pp. 253–278. Bern: Peter Lang.

Adult Education. An Outmoded Concept or What? In Mjelde, L & R. Daly (eds) *Working Knowledge in a Globalizing World. Learning at School,Learning at Work*, 2006. Bern: Peter Lang.

Livingstone, D. W. 1987. Upgrading and Opportunities. In D. W. Livingstone (ed.), *Critical Pedagogy and Culture Power*, pp. 125–136. Cambridge MA: Bergin & Garvey Publishers.

Luria, A. R. 1976. *Cognitive Development: Its Cultural and Social Foundations*. Cambridge MA: Harvard University Press.

Macpherson, C. B. 1962. *The Political Theory of Possessive Individualism*. Oxford and London: Oxford University Press.

Magnussen, T. 1995. Fri for arbeid – om unge vaksne i bygdesamfunn og deira handtering av undersysselsetjing. Bodø: *Nordlandsforskning. Rapport no. 8.*

Marshall, A. 1983. *Changing the Word: The Printing Industry in Transition*. London: Comedia Publishing Corp.

Marx, K. 1967. *Capital, A Critique of Political Economy* Volume 1. New York: International Publishers.

Marx, K & F. Engels 1985: *The German Ideology*. New York: International Publishers.

Maurice, M. & F. Sellier 1979. Societal Analysis of Industrial Relations: A Comparison between France and West Germany. *British Journal of Industrial Relations* XVII, pp. 322–336.

Mayer, C. & I Schutte. 1983. Zur Situation von Mädchen in der Berufsausbildung. In C. Mayer (ed.), *Zur mädchen und Frauen: Beruf und Biographie,* pp. 53–84. München: Verlag Deutsches Jugendinstitut.

Melby, K. 1985. Husmorideologi. In K. Vogt, S. Lie, K. Gundersen & J. Bjørgum, (eds.), *Kvinnenes kulturhistorie fra år 1800 til vår tid*, Vol. 2, pp. 209–212. Oslo: Universitetsforlaget.

Mellin-Olsen, S. 1989. *Kunnskapsformidling: Virksomhetsteoretiske perspektiver.* Bergen: Casper forlag.

Mellin-Olsen, S. & R. Rasmussen. 1975. *I skolens vold.* Oslo: Gyldendal.

Mellin-Olsen, S. & R. Solvang. 1978. *Matematikkundervisning som sosial prosess.* Oslo: NKI forlaget.

Melvold, O. E. 1988. Fattigmansgås på Kampen. *St. Hallvard* No 4, pp. 4–15. Oslo.

Michelsen, S, & H. Høst & J.P. Gitlesen. 1998. Fagopplæring og organisasjon mellom reform og tradisjon. En evaluering av Reform 94. *Arbeid, Historie og Samfunn (AHS) serie B*. Bergen: University of Bergen.

Midtlyng, E. 1998. Mot årtusenskiftet i økt repetisjonstakt. In A. Bernhardsen (ed.), Variert arbeid – fra ensidig til utviklende arbeid. Oslo: Tiden.

Mjåland, S. 1994. Frafall ved Kvadraturen yrkesskole. Masters thesis. Oslo: Statens Yrkespedagogiske Høgskolen (SYH).

Mjelde, L. 1973/1977. Om fravær og frafallsproblemer ved yrkesskolene i Oslo. Cyclostyled paper, Oslo: Sogn Yrkesskole.

Mjelde, L. 1975a. En interesseorganisasjon for yrkeskoleelever og lærlinger blir til. Masters thesis. Institutt for Sosiologi, University of Oslo.

Mjelde, L. 1975b. *Yrkesskoleelever og lærlinger: Proletarer i utdanningssamfunnet.* Oslo: YLI.

Mjelde, L. 1975c. Bygningsarbeid, mannfolkyrke eller? *Kvinnens årbok*, pp. 107–113. Oslo: Pax forlag.

Mjelde, L. 1984a. Skolen som problemskapende faktor for dagens arbeiderungdom. In T. Haaland (ed.), *Ungdom og arbeidsløshet,* pp. 67–88. Oslo: Pax forlag.

Mjelde, L. 1984b Education, Labour Force, the Family: The Connection. *Resources for Feminist Research* 13 (1): 15–16. Toronto: Ontario Institute for Studies in Education (OISE).

Mjelde, L. 1984c. Women and Education (Norway): An annotated bibliography. *Resources for Feminist Research.* pp. 37–38. Toronto: OISE.

Mjelde, L. 1986. *Education and the Labour Market in the North-South Perspective.* Santiago de Chile: Cide Press (Spanish translation).

Mjelde, L. 1987. From Hand to Mind. In D. W. Livingstone (ed.), *Critical Pedagogy and Cultural Power*, pp. 205–221. Cambridge MA: Bergin & Garvey Publishers.

Mjelde, L. 1987: Lærlingordningen I kvinneperspektiv. Oslo: The Norwegian Research Council.

Mjelde, L. 1988. Fra hånd til ånd i yrkesutdanningsperspektiv: Om læring i skole og læring i arbeidsliv. (The Apprenticeship Project 1982–84) Akershus: Høgskolen i Akershus.

Mjelde, L. 1989. Women and Apprenticeship: Gender Contradictions in the Manual Labour Market in Norway. Paper presented at the International Colloquium, University of Antwerp.

Mjelde, L. 1990b. Labour and Learning: The Apprenticeship Program in Norway. *Interchange* 21 (4), pp. 34–48. Toronto: OISE.

Mjelde, L. 1991. *Fra hånd til ånd: Om arbeid og læring i yrkesutdanningsperspektiv.* Oslo: Selskap for Norsk Skolehistorie.

Mjelde, L. 1992. Kjønn, arbeidsdeling og forandring i den grafiske bedriften. In L. Mjelde & A-L. H. Tarrou (eds.), *Arbeidsdeling i en brytningstid*, pp. 27–40. Oslo: Ad Notam Gyldendal.

Mjelde, L. 1993. *Apprenticeship: From Practice to Theory and Back Again.* Joensuu, Finland: University of Joensuu Press.

Mjelde, L. 1994a. Will the Twain Meet? The World of Work and Schooling (Vocational and General) in Relation to Upper Secondary Schooling in Norway. In A. Heikkinen (ed.), *Vocational Education and Culture: European Prospects from History and Life History,* pp. 189–203. Hämeenlinna: University of Tampere Press.

Mjelde, L. 1994b. Will the Twain Meet? The Relationship between the World of Work and the World of Schools. In P. Heywood, K Wain & J Calleja (eds.), *Research into Secondary School Curricula*, pp. 87–96. Amsterdam: Swets & Zeitlinger.
Mjelde, L. 1995. Activity Pedagogy: How Does It Really Work? In A. Heikkinen (ed.), *Vocational Education in the Future*, pp. 131–154. Hämeenlinna: University of Tampere Press.
Mjelde, L. 1996a. The Promise of Alternative Pedagogies – The Case of Workshop Learning. In K. Watson (ed.), *Educational Dilemmas: Debate and Diversity*, vol. 4, pp. 331–340. London: Cassel.
Mjelde, L. 1996 b. Dialogue on Vocational Education. Liv Mjelde and Ronald Sultana. In K. Watson (ed.), *Educational Dilemmas: Debate and Diversity*, vol. 4, pp. 349–354. London: Cassel.
Mjelde, L. 1996c Dinner through Text: The Advent of Domestic Science and Housewife Ideology in Norwegian Education. In A. Heikkinen (ed.), *Gendered History of (Vocational) Education – European Comparisons*, pp. 135–149. Hämeenlinna: University of Tampere Press.
Mjelde, L. 1997a. The Apprenticeship Conundrum. In A. Heikkinen & R. Sultana, (eds.), *Apprenticeship in Europe Towards the Year 2000*, pp. 99–126. Hämeenlinna: University of Tampere Press.
Mjelde, L. 1997b. Hva skal jeg med teori? Det er trykker jeg skal bli. *Norsk Pedagogisk Tidsskrift* 6, pp. 337–349.
Mjelde, L. 2000. Sociological and Philosophical Perspectives on Peace Education. Paper presented at the conference 'Higher Education for Peace', Tromsø: University of Tromsø.
Mjelde, L. 2001. From Factory and Housework to Oil and Caring: Changes in Girls' Education in the Vocational Fields during the Years of Reform 94. In P. Gonon, K. Haefel, A. Heikkinen, & I. Ludwig (eds.) *Gender Perspectives on Vocational Education*, pp. 235–252. Bern: Peter Lang.
Mjelde, L. 2004 Global Restructuring. New Challenges to the Political Economy of Knowledge. In P. Kell, S. Shore & M. Singh. *Adult Education @21st century,* pp. 37–54. New York: Peter Lang.
Mjelde, L. 2004. Changing Work, Changing Households: New Challenges to Masculinities and Femininities in Norwegian Vocational Education. In R. Lakes & P: Carter (eds.), *Globalizing Education for Work: Comparative Perspectives on Gender and the new Economy,* pp. 111–130. London & Mahwah, N.J.: Lawrence Erlbaum Associates.
Mjelde, L. & T. Hammer. 1979. Behandlingsklientell i yrkesskolen. *Helse- og sosialforskning*. Oslo: Sosialdepartement.
Mjelde, L. & A-L. H. Tarrou (eds.) 1992 *Arbeidsdeling i en brytningstid.* Oslo: Ad Notam Gyldendal.
Molander, B. 1993. *Kunskap i handling*. Göteborg: Bokförlaget Daidalos.
Moll, L. C. 1990. *Vygotsky and Education. Instructional Application and Applications of Sociohistorical Psychology*. Cambridge: Cambridge University Press.

Monsen, L. 1997. Innholdsreformen, skolens arbeid med læringsmiljøet. Evaluering of Reform 94. *Arbeidsnotat* 37, Lillehammer.

Moxnes, P. 1981. *Læring og ressursutvikling i arbeidsmiljøet*. Self-published. Oslo.

Mykletun, R. 1975. Elever med handikap i forhold til skolen. En oppsummering av undersøkelser vedrørende ungdomskoleelevers trivsel, stresstilstand og adferdsproblem og mentalhygienske tilstand. Oslo: Skolesjefens kontor.

Nielsen, K. & S. Kvale (eds.) 1999. *Mesterlære: Læring som sosial praksis* (The Master Teacher: Learning as Social Practice). Oslo: Ad Notam Gyldendal.

Nilsen, A. 1998. Great Expectations: Exploring Men's Biographies in Late Modernity. Unpublished manuscript. University of Bergen, Institute of Sociology.

Nilsson, L. 1979. Undervisningsproblem och innlärningssvårigheter inom verkstadsteknisk utbildning. *Rapport* 190. Göteborg: Pedagogiska institutionen, Universitetet i Göteborg.

Nilsson, L. 1981a. *Yrkesundervisning i ljuset av produktionslivets reflexer* Stockholm: Liber förlag.

Nilsson, L. 1981b. Yrkesutbildning i nutidshistoriskt perspektiv. Doctoral dissertation, Göteborg: Universitetet i Göteborg.

Nilsson, L. 1985. *Perspektiv på yrkeslärande i skolmässig form. Förnyelse av yrkeslärande.* Universitetet i Göteborg, Institut for pedagogik.

Nilsson, L. 1992. Fagdidaktikk i yrkespedagogisk perspektiv. In L. Mjelde & A-L. H. Tarrou, eds., *Arbeidsdeling i en brytningstid*, pp. 96–110. Oslo: Ad Notam Gyldendal.

Nilsson, L. 1998. Utmaningar från det yrkesdidaktiska fältet. Conference report. Nordisk yrkespedagogisk konferanse. Akershus: Høgskolen i Akershus.

Nilsson, L. 2000. *Den glömda arbetsuppgiften i samverkan mellan skola och arbetsliv. Om möjligheterna med lärande i arbete.* Stockholm: Utbildningsdepartementet.

Nossum, I. J. 1977. Allmennutdanning – Yrkesutdanning. Masters thesis. Oslo: Pedagogical Research Centre, University of Oslo.

Oakley, Ann (1974) *Housewife.* Harmondsworth: Penguin

Olsen, O. J. 1992. Kvalitet i yrkesutdanningen? Noen mulighetsbetingelser for en erfaringsbasert yrkespedagogikk. *Arbeid, Historie og Samfunn (AHS) serie B, 1992–94.* Bergen: University of Bergen.

Olsen, O. J. (ed.) 1996. Yrkesutdanning og fagopplæring under en moderniserings offensiv. Opplegg for evaluering av Reform 94. *Arbeid, Historie og Samfunn (AHS) serie.* Bergen: University of Bergen.

Olsen, O. J. 2002. Similarities between Systems: Huge Differences between Academic Fields. Reflections on the German Academic Field of Vocational Education from a Norwegian Point of View. In K. Harney et al. (eds.), *Lifelong Learning: One Focus, Different Systems*, pp. 231–246. Frankfurt am Main: Peter Lang.

Olsen, O. J. 2001. A Different Perspective on Equity – The Case of Vocational Education. Introductory paper to Bodø Conference. Bodø: Nordland forskningsinstitutt.

Olsen, O. J. & L. O. Seljestad 1996. Læreplaner og framtidsplaner. Evaluering av Reform 94. *Arbeid, Historie og Samfunn (AHS) serie B, 1997–2.* Bergen: University of Bergen.

Olsen, O. J. et al. 1998. Fagopplæring i omforming. Evaluering av Reform 94. Sluttrapport (Final Report). *Arbeid, Historie og Samfunn (AHS) serien.* Bergen: University of Bergen.

Parelius, N. 1970. *Prost Christian Frost i Veøy. Med erindringer av hans datter Dorothea von der Lippe Christensen.* Molde: Romsdal Kulturvern.

Phillips, A. & B. Taylor. 1986. *Sex and Skill in Waged Work: A Reader.* London: Feminist Review.

Polanyi, M. 1966. *The Tacit Dimension.* London: Routledge & Kegan Paul.

Portelli, L. 1996. A Curriculum History of Domestic Subjects in Malta. Masters thesis, Department of Education, University of Malta.

Postman, N. 1996. *The End of Education. Redefining the Value of School.* New York. Vintage Books.

Prestbakmo, R. 1997. Veiledningssamtalen: En studie av veiledningssamtaler mellom kontaktsykepleier og student. Masters thesis, Akershus: Høgskolen i Akershus.

Prestbakmo, R. 2001. Veiledning og veiledningssamtalen. Kan veiledning gjennom samtaler og ved å vise gjennom eksempler gi den ufaglærte økt kompetanse? Contribution to the Conference "Yrkenes undervisningslære." Akershus: Høgskolen i Akershus.

Ramirez, J. L. 1998. Synekdoke – Om begreppsfenomenologi och om retorik som praktikens kunskapsteori. In O. Eikeland & K. Fossestøl, (eds.), *Kunnskaps-produksjon i endring. Nye erfarings- og organisasjonsformer*, pp.77–92. Oslo: Arbeidsforskningsinstituttet.

Riiber, R. 1997. Reform 94: Fra teori til praksis – hvordan få det til? Masters thesis. Akershus: Høgskolen i Akershus.

Robak, B. 1992. Schriftsetzerinnen und Maschineinfuhrungsstrategien im 19. Jahr-hundert. In A. Wetterer (ed.), *Profession und Geschlecht: Uber die Marginalitæt von Frauen in hochqualifiserten Beruf.* Frankfurt: Campus Verlag.

Roldan, M. 2001. *Development Construction, Work Organization and Gender Hierarchies: Reflections from the Argentine Experience in the 'Transition' to Region-based Capitalism.* Buenos Aires: Flacso/Conicet.

Roldan M. 2006 Information/Knowledge-based Development. Time-Space Config-urations and Engendered Work Organization: Exploring the New International Division of Labour and some Implications for Vocational Education in Argentina. (1990s–2000s) In L. Mjelde & R. Daly (eds.) *Working Knowledge in a Globalizing World. Learning at School, Learning at Work.* Bern: Peter Lang.

Sakslind, R. 1985. Arbeid og utdanning. Omriss av et forskningsfelt. Moralprojektet. *Skriftserie 17.* Bergen: University of Bergen.

Salling-Olesen, H. 1985. *Voksenundervisning – hverdagsliv og erfaring*. København: Unge Pædagoger.
Sandberg, N. & N. Vibe. 1995. *Alle kan ikke bli frisører. Søknad og opptak til videregående opplæring etter Reform 94*. Oslo: NIFU.
Sande, A. 1995. Førr kunn eg aldri tenk meg å heng klea og det gjær eg nå. *Ottar* No. 205, pp. 54–60.
Sandven, J. 1971. Students in General and School-Rejecting Students Compared. *Scandinavian Journal of Educational Research* 15.
Sandvik, G. 1997. *Moderskap og fødselsarbeid. Diskurser i reproduktivt arbeid.* Bergen: Fagbokforlaget.
Sanger, M. 1989. Restructuring as a Gendered Process: Towards a Feminist Political Economy. Paper, Toronto: OISE, University of Toronto.
Schriewer, J. & K. Harney. 1999. Beruflichkeit versus culture technique: Contribution á la semantique du travail en France et en Allemagne. In B.Zimmerman, C. Didry & P. Wagner (eds.), *Le Travail et la nation*, pp. 107–146. Paris: Editions de la Maison des Sciences de l'Homme.
Schøn, D. 1983. *The Reflective Practitioner: How Professionals Think in Action.* New York: Basic Books.
Seccombe, W. 1995. *A Millennium of Family Change: Feudalism to Capitalism in Western Europe*. London: Verso.
Siim, B. 1993. Den kønsopdelte verferdsstat – Ændringer i de politiske kønsrelationer og i kvinders politiske praksis. In K. Nielsen (ed.), *Køn i forandring,* pp. 234–248. København: Forlaget Hyldespjæt.
Skarpenes, Ove 2005. Kunnskapens utvikling og legitimering i videregående skole. Dissertation. Bergen: Institute of Sociology, University of Bergen.
Skinningsrud, T. 1969. Ideologi og skolepolitikk. Masters thesis. Oslo: Pedagogisk forskningsinstitutt, University of Oslo.
Skjønberg, K. 1975. Samordning av den grunnleggende yrkesutdanning. *Yrkes-opplæring* 6, pp. 110–113.
Smith, D. E. 1987. *The Everyday World as Problematic: A Feminist Sociology*. Toronto: University of Toronto Press.
Smith, D. E. 1998. The Underside of Schooling: Restructuring, Privatization and Women's Unpaid Work. *Journal for a Just and Caring Education* 4(1), pp. 11–29.
Smith, D. E. 1999. Telling the Truth after Postmodernism. In D. E. Smith, *Writing the Social: Critique, Theory and Investigations,* pp. 96–130. Toronto: University of Toronto Press.
Sohn-Rethel, A. 1978. *Intellectual and Manual Labour: A Critique of Epistemology*. London: Macmillan Press.
Stang, H. J. 1975. *Ungdom på drift*. Oslo: Universitetsforlaget.
Storstein, E. 1973. *Fra kateterskole til arbeidskole*. Oslo: Pax forlag.
Strauss, S. 1982. *Traitors to the Masculine Cause: The Men's Campaign for Women's Rights*. Wesport, Conn.: Greenwood Press.

Strøm, B.1994. Pedd'n – kulturer på fruktbart gjensyn. Masters thesis. Akershus: Høgskolen i Akershus.
Strømholm, Per 1992. Kristiansand lecture 1992.
Sultana, R. 1992. *Education and National Development. Historical and Critical Perspectives on Vocational Education in Malta.* Malta: Minerva Publications.
Sultana, R. 1996. Between Promise and Possibility: But Will It Really Work? In K. Watson (ed.), *Educational Dilemmas: Debate and Diversity*, vol. 4, pp. 341–348. London: Cassel.
Sunde-Gran, R. 1993. Det eneste konstante er forandring. En undersøkelse om hva kvinnelige rektorer i videregående skole gjør for å fremme skolens utviklings- og læringsarbeid og en analyse av rektorenes opplæringsbehov. Masters thesis. Oslo: Statens Yrkespedagogisk Høgskole (SYH).
Sundli, L. & F. O. Onstad 2003. *Læreres profesjonskunnskap* Oslo: Abstrakt forlag.
Sunnanå, O. 1960. *Georg Kerschensteiner og arbeidskolen.* Oslo: Det Norske Samlaget.
Takala, M. 1992. School Allergy – A Social and Individual Problem. *Acta Universitatis Tamperensis,* Series A, Vol. 335. Tampere.
Tangui, L. 1985. Academic Studies and Technical Education: New Dimensions of an OLD Struggle in the Division of Knowledge. *Sociology of Education* 58: 21–33.
Tarrou, A-L. H. 1988. Challenges in the Education of Teachers of Vocational Subjects and Strategies for Confronting these Challenges. *European Journal of Teacher Education* 11 (2–3), pp. 149–156.
Tarrou, A-L. H. 1995. Komparativ analyse av to fagkulturer i studieretning for håndverks- og industrifag. Doctoral dissertation. Trondheim: Universitetet i Trondheim (NTNU).
Tarrou, A-L. H. 1997. *Yrkespedagogikk og yrkesfaglærerutdanning.* Oslo: Universitetsforlaget.
Telhaug, A. O. 1975. *Vår nye videregående skole.* Oslo: Lærerstudentenes forlag.
Tempte, T. 1982. *Arbetets Ära. Om hantverk, arbete, några rekonstruerade verktyg och maskiner.* Stockholm: Arbeteslivsentrum.
Thirud, E. 1998. Emosjonenes betydning for vår utvikling. Masters thesis. Akershus: Høgskolen i Akershus.
Torvinen, Liisa 1996. Developing Orientation in Business Education. *Nordisk Pedagogikk* No. 3–1996, pp. 144–154.
Toulmin, S. 1978. The Mozart of Psychology *in* New York: *New York Review of Books*. (September 28, p.51).
Ulltveit, G. 1990. *1800-tallets kokebøker. Et tegn i tiden.* Thesis Stabekk: Stabekk Høgskole.
Ulstrup-Engelsen, B. 1999. Utdanningsreformer og læreplansammenheng. *Norsk Pedagogisk Tidsskrift* No. 1, pp. 3–12.
Ulstrup-Engelsen, B. & S. E. Ulvund. 2000. Reform 94, en ulykke for svake elever. *Aftenposten* 16/12/00.
Ve, H. 1977. Sosialisering, kjønn og klasse. In A. M. Berg et al (eds.), *I kvinners bilde. Bidrag til en kvinnesosiologi*, pp. 103–123. Oslo: Pax forlag.

Ve, H. 1981. Class and Gender: Role Model Considerations and Liberations in Advanced Capitalism. *Interchange* 12 (2–3), pp. 151–164.

Vislie, L. 1982 Integration: Its Principle and Practice in *Tidskrift for Nordisk forening for Pedagogisk Forskning. Lund, Sweden Vol 3*, pp. 5–14.

Vogt, G. S. 1950. *Kvinnen i arbeidslivet. Kvinnen i dag.* Oslo: Ernst G. Mortensens forlag.

Voloshinov, V. N. 1973. *Marxism and the Philosophy of Language.* Cambridge MA: Harvard University Press.

Vygotsky, L. 1987. Thought *and Language.* Cambridge MA: MIT Press.

Vygotsky, L. 1978. *Mind in Society: The Development of Higher Psychological Processes.* M. Cole, V. John-Steiner, S. Schribner & E. Soubermann (eds.). Cambridge MA: Harvard University Press.

Wasenden, W. 1995. Yrkesrettet Matematikk. Draft for Arbeids- og litteraturseminar. Akershus: Høgskolen i Akershus.

Wasenden, W. 1997. Matematikkens plass i fagopplæringen innen håndverk og industri. Manuscript. Akershus: Høgskolen i Akershus.

Wasenden, W. 1999. Matematikkens plass i yrkesutdanningen innenfor håndverk og industri. Fra allmenn til yrkesrettet matematikkundervisning. Dissertation. Oslo: University of Oslo: Det utdanningsvitenskapelige fakultet.

Wasenden, W. 2001. *Yrkesretting som pedagogisk prosess.* Akershus: Høgskolen i Akershus.

Wenger, E. 1998. *Learning, Meaning and Identity.* Cambridge: Cambridge University Press.

Willis, P. 1977. *Learning to Labour: How Working Class Kids Get Working Class Jobs.* London: Saxon House.

Wolf, E. R. 1982. *Europe and the Peoples without History.* Berkeley: University of California Press.

Wærness, K. 1991. Vitenskap og husstell i Norge på 1860-tallet. In B. Alver & L. Mikaelsson, (eds.), *Kvinneminnebok til Ida Blom).* Bergen: University of Bergen, Senter for Humanistisk Kvinneforskning.

Waage, J. F. 1995. Et tidsskille i utdanningen av yrkeslærere? *Norsk Pedagogisk Tidsskrift* 4, pp. 152–159.

Østvold, H. 1990. Den videregående skolen og enhetsskoletanken. Lecture for Selskapet for Norsk skolehistorie, October 25, 1990.

## Official European Documents

OECD 2003. *Education at a Glance. OECD indicators 2003* Paris: OECD-Publications.

OECD 2004a. *Education at a Glance. OECD educators 2004* Paris: OECD-Publications.
OECD 2004 b. *Learning for Tomorrow's World. First results from Pisa 2003* Paris: OECD Publications.
OECD 2004c. Completing the Foundation for Lifelong Learning. An OECD survey of Upper Secondary Schools. Paris: OECD Publications.

## Official Norwegian Documents

Abbrevations:

| | |
|---|---|
| (NOU) | Norges Offentlige Utredninger: Norway's Official Documents |
| (OT PROP) | (Odelstingsproposisjon): Parliamentary Proposals |
| Stortingsmelding: | White Paper |

## Norwegian Ministry of Education (KUF: Kirke og Utdanningsdepartementet) Parliamentary Acts on Education

1941 Skolekjøkkensaken i Norge gjennom 50 år. (On the Matter of the School Kitchen in Norway over 50 Years). Pamphlet.
1945 Lov om yrkeskoler for Håndverk og industri. (Act on Vocational Schools for Crafts and Industry), implementing the Vocational School Act of 1940.
1950 Lærlingloven (The *Apprenticeship Act*).
1965 Plan for den videre utbygging av yrkeskolen for håndverk og industri for perioden 1965–1971) [A country-wide plan for further construction of vocational schools for crafts and industry, commerce and office work etc. for the period 1965–71 ( White Paper No. 7).
*Act of March 1st*, 1940 respecting vocational training, schools for handicrafts and industry as subsequently amended, last by Act of 3rd May 1963.
1974–75 *Om videregående opplæring*. (On Upper Secondary Education). White Paper No. 44.
1974 *Lov om videregående opplæring av 21. juni 1974*. (Act of 21 June 1974 Concerning the Upper Secondary School). Constituted January 1. 1976.

1975 *Alternativ opplæring i ungdomsskolen* (Alternative Training in Secondary Schooling. (White Paper No 8).
1976 *Yrkesutdanning i skole og arbeidsliv.* (Vocational Education in School and Working- Life) (White Paper No 31).
1980 *Lov om opplæring i arbeidslivet av 23 Mai* (Act on Education in Working life May 23).
1980 *Utdanning og arbeid.* (Education and Work) White Paper No 35.
1982 Vocational Training in Norway. KUF: Pamphlet.
1988 *Med viten og vilje.* (With Knowledge and Intent.) White Paper No 28.
1989 Rådet for fagopplæring i Arbeidslivet: Årsmelding. (The Council on Apprenticeship Training in Working Life. Annual Report).
1991 Veien videre til studie- og yrkeskompetanse for alle. (The Road to further Studies and Job Competence for All. [Blegen Committee]). NOU No. 4.
1991/92 *Kunnskap og kyndighet. Om visse sider ved videregående opplæring.* (Knowledge and Skill: On Certain Aspects of Upper Secondary Education.) White Paper No. 33.
1992 The Changing Role of Vocational and Technical Education and Training. Report to OECD.
1996–1997 *Om lærlingsituasjonen.* (On the Apprenticeship situation) White paper No. 22.
1998–1999 *Videregående opplæring.* (Further Education) White paper No. 32.
2004 *Kultur for læring* (Culture for Learning). White Paper No. 30.
2005 Utdanningsspeilet. Analyse av grunnskole og videregående opplæring i Norge. Oslo: Utdanningsdirektoratet.

## Norwegian Ministry of Family Affairs

1978 *Lov om likestilling mellom kjønnene* (Law on Equality between the Sexes).
1991 Mannsrolleutvalgets sluttrapport. (Final report from the Commision on the Male Role.) NOU No. 3.

# Index

# studien zur berufs- und weiterbildung
# studies in vocational and continuing education

**herausgegeben von / edited by**
**philipp gonon & anja heikkinen**

Das Ziel dieser Reihe ist es, kritische, historische und international vergleichende Forschung im Bereich der Berufs- und Weiterbildung und der Personalentwicklung aus pädagogischer, organisatorischer, ökonomischer und sozialer Perspektive zu diskutieren. Sie will die neuesten Forschungsergebnisse in der heutigen Bildungsreform und -praxis in einem kulturübergreifenden Kontext präsentieren. Aspekte zur Frauen- und Geschlechterforschung sollen einen Schwerpunkt der Publikationen bilden.

Die Reihe wird vom Internationalen Netzwerk "VET and Culture" (Vocational Education and Training and Culture) unterstützt. Die Herausgeber laden namhafte Forscher aus Europa und anderen Kontinenten ein, mit eigenen Veröffentlichungen zum Profil der Reihe beizutragen. In der Reihe werden sowohl Monographien wie Konferenzbeiträge in deutscher und englischer Sprache veröffentlicht.

The aim of this series is to present critical, historical and comparative research in the field of vocational and continuing education and human research development, seen from a pedagogical, organisational, economic and societal perspective. It discusses the implications of latest research to contemporary reform policies and practices. One central issue reflected in all publications is gender. A basic feature of all volumes is their cross-cultural approach.

The series has a firm basis in the international research network "VET and Culture" (Vocational Education and Training and Culture) and the editors invite distinguished researchers from Europe and other continents to contribute to the series. *Studies in vocational and continuing education* include monographs and proceedings in German or English.

Vol. 1 Antony Lindgren & Anja Heikkinen (eds)
Social Competences in Vocational and Continuing Education
2004. 256 S. ISBN 3-03910-345-8 / US-ISBN 0-8204-7013-9

Vol. 2 Liv Mjelde
The Magical Properties of Workshop Learning
2006. 230 S. ISBN 3-03910-348-2 / US-ISBN 0-8204-7014-7

Vol. 3 Liv Mjelde & Richard Daly (eds)
Working Knowledge in a Globalizing World
From Work to Learning, from Learning to Work
2006. 406 S. ISBN 3-03910-974-X / 0-8204-8364-8

Antony Lindgren / Anja Heikkinen (eds.)

# Social Competences in Vocational and Continuing Education

*Bern, Berlin, Bruxelles, Frankfurt am Main, New York, Oxford, Wien, 2004.*
*256 pp., 6 fig.*
*Studies in Vocational and Continuing Education. Vol. 1*
*Edited by Philipp Gonon and Anja Heikkinen*
*ISBN 3-03910-345-8 / US-ISBN 0-8204-7013-9 pb.*
*sFr. 68.– / €* 46.90 / €** 43.80 / £ 31.– / US-$ 52.95*

* includes VAT – only valid for Germany and Austria ** does not include VAT

Social competences have played a crucial role in the international search for generic, over-arching skills, key qualifications and core competences since the 1970s. By the end of 1990, social cohesion and integration had gained new momentum in this discourse because of their importance for the functioning of global market economy and industries. Moreover, the concept of social capital affects and changes the role of social competences in vocational and continuing education.

This volume presents a collection of papers which reflect and describe these changes and their political, economical and pedagogical backgrounds and implications. The topics include economisation of social competences, social competences as key qualifications for employability and entrepreneurship, social challenges in eroding welfare societies, gender and social competences, and the ideological and economical context of the social competences discourse.

Wiht contributions by: Philipp Gonon – Anja Heikkinen – Antony Lindgren – – Lorenz Lassnigg – Matthias Vonken – Beatrix Niemeyer – Liv Mjelde – Håkon Høst – Svein Michelsen – Rudolf Husemann – Katrin Kraus.

The Editors: Antony Lindgren is an Associate professor and senior lecturer in sociology at Luleå University of Technology, Sweden. He lectures on political sociology, sociological theory, regional studies and the philosophy of science and is currently researching on working conditions in «the new service-jobs» and on vocational education.

Anja Heikkinen is a professor of adult education at the University of Jyväskylä, Finland. Her main research areas are historical, cultural and gender aspects of education, primarily in vocational and continuing education. She has been active for years in various European projects and international networks, which promote cross-cultural collaboration in teaching and researching vocational and continuing education.

**PETER LANG**
Bern · Berlin · Bruxelles · Frankfurt am Main · New York · Oxford · Wien

Liv Mjelde / Richard Daly (eds)

**Working Knowledge in a Globalizing World**

From Work to Learning, from Learning to Work

*Bern, Berlin, Bruxelles, Frankfurt am Main, New York, Oxford, Wien, 2006. 406 pp.*
*Studies in Vocational and Continuing Education. Vol. 3*
*Edited by Philipp Gonon and Anja Heikkinen*
*ISBN 3-03910-974-X / US-ISBN 0-8204-8364-8 pb.*
*sFr. 92.– / €* 63.10 / €** 59.– / £ 41.30 / US-$ 70.95*

* includes VAT – only valid for Germany and Austria ** does not include VAT

Vocational education is an interface between practical and theoretical knowledge involving both work-related general knowledge and practical knowledge generated at work. The contributions cover many features of VET (Vocational Education and Training) in a global world. Part one examines VET's work-relatedness as education marked by social or group (rather than individual) dynamics, and is inductive and practice-oriented.

The second part of this volume critically examines features of vocational education policy that are central to a number of present-day global social and economic concerns in light of changes in apprenticeship policies, information technology, structural adjustment, crises in youth culture, and shifting regional political and economic agendas. Global VET concerns are presented from national conditions of Argentina, Australia, Austria, Canada, Cuba, Denmark, Germany, Norway, South Africa, Spain, Sweden, Switzerland and the USA.

With contributions by: Vibe Aarkrog – Faizul Bhyat – Jeanne Gamble – Garnet Grosjean – Tony Irizar – Adita Chiappy – Liv Mjelde – Antje Barabasch – Patricia A. Carter – Thomas Deissinger – Philipp Gonon – Peter Kell – Katrin Kraus – Richard D. Lakes – Lorenz Lassnigg – Antony Lindgren – Martha Roldán – Anne Smehaugen – Manfred Wahle – Markus Weil.

The Editors: Liv Mjelde, a sociologist specialised in sociology of education, is Professor of Vocational Pedagogy, Akershus University College, Norway. Her research interests include the social organisation of knowledge as well as comparative research into gendered work, education and the labour market.

Richard Daly is a social anthropologist who has researched and published on the social division of knowledge and Canadian Aboriginal rights. He has worked in the field of Aboriginal education.

FSC
www.fsc.org
MIX
Papier | Fördert gute Waldnutzung
FSC® C083411

Kolibri 360 GmbH
Ferdinand-Jühlke-Straße 7
99095 Erfurt, Deutschland
produktsicherheit@kolibri360.de